Life Together

Life Together

Dietrich Bonhoeffer

Translated by Daniel W. Bloesch

Introduction by Geffrey B. Kelly

Supplemental Material by Victoria J. Barnett

Fortress Press
Minneapolis

LIFE TOGETHER

Dietrich Bonhoeffer Works—Reader's Edition

Cover image: Portrait of Bonhoeffer by Paul Huet

Cover design: Laurie Ingram

Library of Congress Cataloging-in-Publication Data

Print ISBN: 978-1-5064-0276-5

eBook ISBN: 978-1-5064-0277-2

The paper used in this publication meets the minimum requirements of American National Standard for Information Sciences — Permanence of Paper for Printed Library Materials, ANSI Z329.48-1984.

Manufactured in the U.S.A.

This book was produced using Pressbooks.com, and PDF rendering was done by PrinceXML.

Contents

Editor's Introduction to the Reader's Edition of *Life Together*

Geffrey B. Kelly

From his earliest days at Humboldt University in Berlin, Dietrich Bonhoeffer desired to shape and live in a Christian faith community. He was intrigued by the mystery of how God in Jesus becomes present among those who profess their faith together and celebrate their oneness with the Lord through the nurturing words of the gospel and their common worship. He was already exploring such possibilities with his Berlin University students in 1931.

The intellectual underpinnings of Bonhoeffer's convictions on life in a Christian faith community can be traced to his early works *Sanctorum Communio* and *Act and Being*, which undergirded his interpretation of the church as a primary form of God's self-revelation. In both works Bonhoeffer contended that communities of faith in Christ must assume concrete form in the world in order to radiate the presence of God credibly and effectively, and to live in service to those in need. The will of God is expressed through the words spoken to human beings and their communities of faith. Bonhoeffer insisted that Christian communities could not allow God's will to be merely an abstract idea or smothered in institutional, dogmatic, or biblical reductionism. His spiritual classics *Discipleship* and *Life Together* were thus given a realistic embodiment in their most tangible form, the Christian community.

Bonhoeffer sought to explain these theological insights and his commitment to church ministry and its sacramental embodiment in clear language that reflected the lived reality of people who were drawn together through the faith they shared. In his foundational study of church, *Sanctorum Communio*, he sought to integrate the confession of faith in the presence of Jesus Christ with the community's structuring of that presence. Bonhoeffer described the church with the memorable phrase, "Christ existing as the church community."[1]

Life Together deals with the nature of this Christ-centered community: the life of Christians living together, united in service to and for one another through prayer, the practice of confession, and partaking of the Lord's Supper. It presupposes the Christo-ecclesiological foundation of *Sanctorum Communio*. In *Life Together*, Christians in Christ are moved to do what they would be unable to accomplish without Jesus: to live together and offer one another their self-giving love in a prayerful, compassionate, and caring community. Christ is proclaimed present in this community as the Word, gracing Christians to go beyond the superficial, often self-centered relationships of their everyday associations and to move toward a more intimate sense of what it means to be Christ to others, and to love others as Christ as loved them.

Life Together was not simply a devotional text, however; it was

---

1. See *Sanctorum Communio* (Bonhoeffer Works volume 1), 121 and 198.

Bonhoeffer's own reflection on his attempt to create such a community with his seminarians in Finkenwalde from 1935 to 1937. Finkenwalde was one of five Confessing Church seminaries that emerged after the pro-Nazi Reich bishop, Ludwig Müller, ordered the closing of preachers' seminaries in the Old Prussian Union church in March 1934. Determined to continue training seminarians, Confessing Church leaders in Prussia invited Bonhoeffer in July 1934 to direct a seminary in Brandenburg. At the Dahlem Synod of October 1934 the radical wing of the Confessing Church declared its independence from the official church. In Bonhoeffer's eyes, the official church—led by openly pro-Nazi church leaders like Müller and by overly cautious bishops who opted for compromise with these officials—had abandoned all pretense of being a true Christian church. The break at Dahlem meant that seminarians who were committed to the Confessing Church were "illegal" in the eyes of the official church, barred from ordination and the ministry, and thus had to be trained for the ministry at privately established seminaries by Confessing pastors and theologians.

Even before the Dahlem Synod, Bonhoeffer had been thinking of a different model for theological education. While still in London he wrote his Swiss friend, Erwin Sutz, that the training of young seminarians belonged not in the university, but "entirely in church monastic schools, where the pure doctrine, the Sermon on the Mount, and worship are taken seriously—which for all three of these things is simply not the case at the university and under the present circumstances is impossible."[2] While in England, he visited several Anglican communities and monasteries to become acquainted with their methods and routines. Bonhoeffer returned to Germany in April 1935 and took up his new duties in June.

---

2. Letter from London, September 11, 1934, in *London: 1933-1935* (Bonhoeffer Works volume 13, p. 217).

Life Together is a studious exposition of the Christian community of seminarians whom he trained in Finkenwalde. Bonhoeffer instructed them about ministry, prayer life, the spiritual love and the brotherhood that they should extend to one another, unselfish service to those in need, the need for meditation on the Word of God and common worship. It is a detailed account of how Bonhoeffer and his seminarians became a community of brothers bonded through their common faith and mutual service in preparation for their ministry. Bonhoeffer adamantly contended that the strength and objectivity to preach the Word of the Gospels came from the common life of the seminarians, as opposed to pastoral actions as isolated individuals, and he argued that Christian life and the faith can never be lived in the abstract. In his view, the very nature of the church community demanded renunciation of clerical privileges and full availability for service to the people entrusted to their care. Finally, he envisaged that in their daily routine the seminarians would enjoy a simple common life in a schedule of daily prayer and meditation, theological studies, mutual service to one another, and worship. During the period of their life together, they would have to learn "how to lead a community life in daily and strict obedience to the will of Christ Jesus, in the practice of the humblest and noblest service one Christian brother can perform for another. They must learn to recognize the strength and liberation to be found in their brotherly service and their life together in a Christian community. Second, they have to learn to serve the truth alone in their study of the Bible and its interpretation in their sermons and instruction."[3]

Jesus's self-sacrificing love and daring actions on behalf of his followers, as portrayed in Bonhoeffer's earliest writings, were the

---

3. Letter of June 27, 1936, to Wolfgang Staemmler, director of the Saxon preachers' seminary in Frankfurt, in *Theological Education at Finkenwalde: 1935-1937* (Bonhoeffer Works volume 14, p. 196).

Christocentric foundations for the ecclesiology of *Life Together*. Bonhoeffer's entire approach to the community life portrayed in *Life Together* was centered on how Jesus Christ continues to be present in the world through his followers, graced by the Holy Spirit to continue what he began during his incarnational presence among them. At Finkenwalde, Bonhoeffer and the seminarians he directed came to depend on this sense of Jesus' continuing presence among them, nurtured by their strong faith in Jesus Christ, manifest in the biblical word on which they meditated daily and their common worship. Their relationship to each other was augmented through their intercessory prayers for one another and for those in need beyond the seminary walls. As Bonhoeffer had stressed in *Sanctorum Communio*, in their compassion and care for each other the seminarians came to be not only *with* one another, but more especially to live *for* one another.[4] Being *for* one another leads to an attitude that is more clearly Christ-like: "Whoever lives in love is Christ in relation to the neighbor." For Bonhoeffer this meant that "Christians can and ought to act like Christ, they ought to bear the burdens and sufferings of the neighbor." Citing Luther, he wrote: "'You must open your heart to the weaknesses and needs of others as if they were your own, and offer your means as if they were theirs, just as Christ does for you in the sacrament.'"[5]

One reason that readers of *Life Together* find it so compelling is its portrayal of the inner strength and intensity of Bonhoeffer's relationship with Jesus Christ as developed in the practical everyday life of the Christian community he directed. Bonhoeffer's account of the community-sustained spiritual life at Finkenwalde was not a mere

---

4. *Sanctorum Communio* (Bonhoeffer Works volume 1), 88. Bonhoeffer makes this distinction to illustrate the differences that can exist in social forms in communities; italics mine.
5. Ibid., 178. Bonhoeffer uses this distinction to show the extent to which being for one another in community is more demanding and closer to the example of Jesus Christ.

reminiscence about an agreeable, idyllic experience of a like-minded group of young seminarians; he intended to share the experience with others as a model for creating forms of church community in a Germany torn apart during the destructive years of the Hitler dictatorship. With vivid memories of how he and his seminarians were able to form a supportive community in Finkenwalde, Bonhoeffer wrote that what they accomplished could become a possibility for the church as a whole—in fact such communities could become a genuine mission for the church at large.[6]

Ironically, it was the Gestapo that made this remarkable book possible. On September 28, 1937, the Gestapo closed Finkenwalde after an order by Heinrich Himmler that declared all the Confessing Church seminaries illegal. Bonhoeffer continued to train and mentor his seminarians in "underground pastorates" scattered throughout the provinces around Berlin. These "underground pastorates" were essentially small churches aligned with the Confessing Church. Bonhoeffer stayed in regular contact with the seminarians through circular letters and visitations. Despite these efforts, their period of "life together" had ended.

The Writing of *Life Together*

Bonhoeffer had been reluctant to publicize the Finkenwalde "experiment," feeling that the time was not ripe. With the closing of the seminary at Finkenwalde and the dispersal of his seminarians, however, Bonhoeffer felt compelled not only to record for posterity the daily regimen and its rationale, but also to express his conviction that the worldwide church itself needed to promote a sense of community if it was to have new life.

Bonhoeffer and his closest friend, Eberhard Bethge, who had been

---

6. See Bonhoeffer's Preface to this volume, p. 1.

an active part of the Finkenwalde community, journeyed to Göttingen in late September 1938 to the empty home of Bonhoeffer's twin sister, Sabine, and her husband Gerhard Leibholz, a professor of law at the university and a baptized Christian of Jewish descent who had been dismissed from his professorship. Bonhoeffer and Bethge had helped the Leibholz family escape from Germany to Switzerland. Now Bonhoeffer sat at Leibholz's desk and worked on the manuscript almost nonstop with only a few breaks.

The work was overshadowed by Bonhoeffer's disappointment in the Confessing Church leadership, his growing awareness that war was imminent, and his first encounters with resistance figures through his brother-in-law Hans von Dohnanyi. The oath of personal allegiance to Hitler taken by a majority of the Confessing Church pastors filled Bonhoeffer with frustration and added to his urgency to complete the book. Hitler's annexation of the Sudetenland, the official order in November that Bonhoeffer register for the military, and the November "Kristallnacht" pogroms amplified his sense that he was working against the clock.

The political-religious situation was reflected in several comments in the first section of the book, such as Bonhoeffer's remark that "the Christian cannot simply take for granted the privilege of living among other Christians," adding that Christians belong "in the midst of enemies. There they find their mission, their work" (p. 3). If we can extrapolate from *Life Together*, that "mission" and "work" seemed to be the infusion of new life and a new sense of Christian community into a church grown cowardly and less than Christ-like under the spell of the Hitler dictatorship.

Life Together was published in 1939 as a theological monograph.[7] Within one year it went into its fourth printing. Since its first

---

7. It was published as part of *Theologische Existenz heute* (Theological existence today), Volume 61.

publication in English in 1954 by Harper and Row, the previous translation of *Life Together* has gone through twenty-three reprintings. The new Bonhoeffer Works translation published in this Reader's Edition has corrected the errors of the previous translations and follows Bonhoeffer's text more closely.

The Structure of *Life Together*

The structure of *Life Together* follows the daily schedule kept at Finkenwalde, with sections on "Community," "The Day Together," "The Day Alone," "Service," and "Confession and the Lord's Supper."

Community

Bonhoeffer began by quoting Psalm 133: "How very good and pleasant it is when brothers live together in unity," emphasizing the strength of the Christian community against those adversaries who would destroy them. Quoting Luther, he reminded his seminarians that their community life was set in the midst of vicious enemies bent on their destruction and that their protection and power would emanate from the "physical presence of other Christians." He analyzed the dangerous elements that eroded community life, warning the seminarians against the "wishful thinking" so distant from the lived reality (p. 12). The reality of their fidelity to Jesus Christ would give them courage to endure the many conflicts that could crop up in any community that sought to follow the path set by Jesus Christ.

Bonhoeffer then wrote about the nature of the love that was the binding force in the Christian community, criticizing "purely emotional love," which when unexamined vitiated the call of Christ to an agapeic love that was without preset conditions. Unlike calculating, manipulative, self-serving "emotional" love, the spiritual love Bonhoeffer advocated was deferential, humble, and unconditional. Spiritual love was agapeic, like the love that Jesus Christ extended to all. Christians should recognize the true image of the other person from the perspective of Christ himself, resisting all attempts to coerce and dominate others rather than loving them for who they are: as those for whom Christ became incarnate among his people and with whom Christ became bonded in their brotherly love. In Christian community there was "access to one another, joy in one another, community with one another through Christ alone" (p. 23).

The Day Together

In the second section Bonhoeffer emphasized the need for daily structure. The day of shared faith began early, with communal worship in which they sang hymns, read the scriptures, and prayed aloud, often with one person taking the lead. Bonhoeffer wanted the seminarians to consider this time early in the morning as sacred, during which they could experience anew the mediation of Jesus Christ and the enlightenment of God's Word. They prayed the Psalms together as the Prayer of Christ himself. The beginning of the day was not to be burdened by the concerns they would face during the busy day. The reading of the scriptures together and their singing, conjoined to their meditation and table fellowship, were moments that by their very routine contributed to their bonding in a Christ-centered love. As the day ended they gathered again for the evening breaking of bread together and the final worship service, which included reconciliation and mutual forgiveness. "When could we ever have a deeper awareness of God's power and working than in the hour when we lay aside our own work and entrust ourselves to God's faithful hands?" (p. 54).

The Day Alone

Bonhoeffer realized that many seek community because they fear loneliness, cannot endure being alone, cannot cope with life on their own, or have been scarred by bad experiences and seek help in the company of others. He believed that such persons are not called to live their faith in a Christian faith community, where the day together is marked by Christ's call to be alone in meditative prayer. There is a reality to moments of solitude within the Christian community, often occurring in the realization that one will experience the importance of solitude in obeying God's call, taking up Christ's cross, being alone in prayer, and being alone in death in the Lord. From that solitude and the sense of being alone with Christ, Bonhoeffer believed Christians could find strength in complementary togetherness, living more alertly to the presence of Christ within a Christian community.

Bonhoeffer emphasized: "Whoever cannot be alone should beware of community" (p. 57). When persons in community live closely together in a confined space and cannot give each other the necessary quiet, the need arises for periods of quiet and silence. The solitude of such moments is a needed complement to the many moments in the daily routine when one longs for space and quiet. Three factors in a Christian faith community require solitude: meditation on the scriptures, prayer, and intercession. All three have their place in the daily period of meditation. Bonhoeffer viewed intercessory prayer as an outcome of solitude but also as providing an amazing thrill, since through intercessory prayer, Christians bring one another into the presence of God. Bonhoeffer called intercessory prayer God's gift of grace for every Christian community. Realizing that the early morning hours were the best time for "being alone" in the solitude of meditation and intercessory prayer, he concluded that this solitude, together with the sharing in the love of Christ in the daily routine of being together, would prove a "daily source of new joy in God and in the Christian community" (p. 67).

Service to One Another

The diversity of those who comprise the Christian faith community is an important aspect of God's blessings. The presence of Christians to one another is a visible way in which Christ is enfleshed anew. Everyone contributes to the dynamics of living together in harmony—the talented and the untalented, the devout and those less devout, the sociable and the loners. Since the inevitable judgments about character and classifications of people are dangerous to the soul of the community, Bonhoeffer counseled the brothers to rejoice in the opportunity this presented to strengthen their bonds with one another. The strength of their community lay in their concern and care for their weakest brothers.

Bonhoeffer hoped to integrate this diversity into a strengthened faithfulness to the presence of Jesus Christ among them through the daily schedule of service, common worship, scripture reading, and table fellowship, growing in their love for one another and into the image of Jesus Christ among them. Bonhoeffer focused on three particular kinds of service that promoted this growth. First came the service of listening to one another, especially when people crave nothing more than listening to their problems. If one can't listen to another in need, Bonhoeffer asked, how can he listen to God? The second was active helpfulness: "Nobody is too good for the lowest service," he wrote. "Those who worry about the loss of time entailed by such small external acts of helpfulness are usually taking their own work too seriously" (p. 78). Even the smallest task could remind the brothers that God's ways were not always their ways. Finally, Bonhoeffer spoke of the service of forbearance, drawing from Paul's advice: "Bear one another's burdens, and in this way you will fulfill the law of Christ" (Gal. 6:2). Bonhoeffer understood that forbearance is how God draws Christians into a serving community marked by its very diversity. The strong should help the weak, the healthy help those who are ill, the talented help the untalented, the righteous help the sinner, always in a Christ-like manner. Service deepens the personal and spiritual relationships that are so integral to the common life of the Christian community.

Confession and the Lord's Supper

In the last segment of *Life Together*, Bonhoeffer emphasized the need for Christians to confess their sins to one another. The call to confession is essential to those living together that they might confront their sins directly, particularly sins that have a direct impact on community well-being. On the practical level Bonhoeffer saw this as an opportunity for Christians to drop their masks, pretenses, and denials, and to acknowledge who they are in God's sight. In the act of confession, members of the community could become Christ for one another. The reconciliation that comes through having sins forgiven is the best preparation for those who desire to receive the body and blood of Jesus Christ and, through the Lord's Supper, to renew their commitment to one another. Reconciled in their hearts and with one another, the community received the gift of Jesus' body and blood, receiving new life and salvation. "Here the community has reached its goal. Here joy in Christ and Christ's community is complete. The life together of Christians under the Word has reached its fulfillment in the sacrament" (p. 99).

> An idealistic view of human acceptance of others' sins — a purity expected that rarely exists — See Puritan life in America!

Bonhoeffer's Hope for the Future of Christian Faith Communities in the Manner of *Life Together*

As Bonhoeffer wrote in his Preface to *Life Together*, he hoped that the Finkenwalde model of community could become a possibility for the church as a whole, a "mission entrusted to the Church" (p. 1). The Christian church, he believed, urgently needed to find different ways to be, to follow Christ along the lines of Jesus' gospel. Only thus could it resist the political ideology that had successfully gained the allegiance of most churchgoers in Nazi Germany.

While this book was a timely message to the churches of Germany during the turbulent 1930s, its lasting popularity illustrates the timelessness of Bonhoeffer's inspiring vision for a genuine Christian life together.

Community

Daily Structure

Meditation
Prayer
Intercession

Confession

Preface

The subject matter I am presenting here is such that any further development can take place only through a common effort. We are not dealing with a concern of some private circles but with a mission entrusted to the church. Because of this, we are not searching for more or less haphazard individual solutions to a problem. This is, rather, a responsibility to be undertaken by the church as a whole. There is a hesitation evident in the way this task has been handled. Only recently has it been understood at all. But this hesitation must give way to the willingness of the church to assist in the work. The variety of new ecclesial forms of community makes it necessary to enlist the vigilant cooperation of every responsible party. The following remarks are intended to provide only one individual contribution toward answering the extensive questions that have been raised thereby. As much as possible, may these comments help to clarify this experience and put it into practice.

Community

"How very good and pleasant it is when kindred live together in unity!" (Ps. 133:1) In what follows we will take a look at several directions and principles that the Holy Scriptures give us for life together [gemeinsame Leben] under the Word.

The Christian cannot simply take for granted the privilege of living among other Christians. Jesus Christ lived in the midst of his enemies. In the end all his disciples abandoned him. On the cross he was all alone, surrounded by criminals and the jeering crowds. He had come for the express purpose of bringing peace to the enemies of God. So Christians, too, belong not in the seclusion of a cloistered life but in the midst of enemies. There they find their mission, their work. "To rule is to be in the midst of your enemies. And whoever will not suffer this does not want to be part of the rule of Christ; such a person wants to be among friends and sit among the roses and lilies, not with the bad people but the religious people. O you blasphemers and betrayers of Christ! If Christ had done what you are doing, who would ever have been saved?" (Luther).

"Though I scattered them among the nations, yet in far countries they shall remember me" (Zech. 10:9). According to God's will, the Christian church is a scattered people, scattered like seed "to all the kingdoms of the earth" (Deut. 28:25). That is the curse and its promise. God's people must live in distant lands among the unbelievers, but they will be the seed of the kingdom of God in all the world.

"I will . . . gather them in. For I have redeemed them, . . . and they shall . . . return" (Zech. 10:8–9). When will that happen? It has happened in Jesus Christ, who died "to gather into one the dispersed children of God" (John 11:52), and ultimately it will take place visibly at the end of time when the angels of God will gather God's elect from the four winds, from one end of heaven to the other (Matt. 24:31). Until then, God's people remain scattered, held together in Jesus Christ alone, having become one because they remember *him* in the distant lands, spread out among the unbelievers.

Thus in the period between the death of Christ and the day of judgment, when Christians are allowed to live here in visible community with other Christians, we have merely a gracious anticipation of the end time. It is by God's grace that a congregation is permitted to gather visibly around God's word and sacrament in this world. Not all Christians partake of this grace. The imprisoned, the sick, the lonely who live in the diaspora, the proclaimers of the gospel in heathen lands stand alone. They know that visible community is grace. They pray with the psalmist: "I went with the throng, and led them in procession to the house of God, with glad shouts and songs of thanksgiving, a multitude keeping festival" (Ps. 42:5). But they remain alone in distant lands, a scattered seed according to God's will. Yet what is denied them as a visible experience they grasp more ardently in faith. Hence "in the Spirit on the Lord's Day" (Rev. 1:10) the exiled disciple of the Lord, John the author of the Apocalypse, celebrates the worship of heaven with its congregations in the loneliness of the Island of Patmos. He sees the seven lampstands that are the congregations, the seven stars that are the angels of the congregations, and in the midst and above it all, the Son of Man, Jesus Christ, in his great glory as the risen one. He strengthens and comforts John by his word. That is the heavenly community in which the exile participates on the day of his Lord's resurrection.

The physical presence of other Christians is a source of incomparable joy and strength to the believer. With great yearning the imprisoned apostle Paul calls his "beloved son in the faith," Timothy, to come to him in prison in the last days of his life. He wants to see him again and have him near. Paul has not forgotten the tears Timothy shed during their final parting (2 Tim. 1:4). Thinking of the congregation in Thessalonica, Paul prays "night and day . . . most earnestly that we may see you face to face" (1 Thess. 3:10). The aged John knows his joy in his own people will only be complete when he can come to them and speak to them face to face instead of using paper and ink (2 John 12). The believer need not feel any shame when yearning for the physical presence of other Christians, as if one were still living too much in the flesh. A human being is created as a body; the Son of God appeared on earth in the body for our sake and was raised in the body. In the sacrament the believer receives the Lord Christ in the body, and the resurrection of the dead will bring about the perfected community of God's spiritual-physical creatures. Therefore, the believer praises the Creator, the Reconciler and the Redeemer, God the Father, Son and Holy Spirit, for the bodily presence of the other Christian. The prisoner, the sick person, the Christian living in the diaspora recognizes in the nearness of a fellow Christian a physical sign of the gracious presence of the triune God. In their loneliness, both the visitor and the one visited recognize in each other the Christ who is present in the body. They receive and meet each other as one meets the Lord, in reverence, humility, and joy. They receive each other's blessings as the blessing of the Lord Jesus Christ. But if there is so much happiness and joy even in a single encounter of one Christian with another, what inexhaustible riches must invariably open up for those who by God's will are privileged to live in daily community life with other Christians! Of course, what is an inexpressible blessing from God for the lonely individual is easily disregarded and trampled under foot by those who receive the gift every day. It is easily forgotten that the community of Christians is a gift of grace from the kingdom of God, a gift that can be taken from us any day—that the time still separating us from the most profound loneliness may be brief indeed. Therefore, let those who until now have had the privilege of living a Christian life together with other Christians praise God's grace from the bottom of their hearts. Let them thank God on their knees and realize: it is grace, nothing but grace, that we are still permitted to live in the community of Christians today.

The measure with which God gives the gift of visible community is varied. Christians who live dispersed from one another are comforted by a brief visit of another Christian, a prayer together, and another Christian's blessing. Indeed, they are strengthened by letters written by the hands of other Christians. Paul's greetings in his letters written in his own hand were no doubt tokens of such community. Others are given the gift on Sundays of the community of the worship service. Still others have the privilege of living a Christian life in the community of their families. Before their ordination young seminarians receive the gift of a common life with their brothers for a certain length of time. Among serious Christians in congregations today there is a growing desire to meet together with other Christians during the midday break from work for life together under the Word. Life together is again being understood by Christians today as the grace that it is, as the extraordinary aspect, the "roses and lilies" of the Christian life (Luther).

Christian community means community through Jesus Christ and in Jesus Christ. There is no Christian community that is more than this, and none that is less than this. Whether it be a brief, single encounter or the daily community of many years, Christian community is solely this. We belong to one another only through and in Jesus Christ.

What does that mean? It means, *first*, that a Christian needs others for the sake of Jesus Christ. It means, *second*, that a Christian comes to others only through Jesus Christ. It means, *third*, that from eternity we have been chosen in Jesus Christ, accepted in time, and united for eternity.

First, Christians are persons who no longer seek their salvation, their deliverance, their justification in themselves, but in Jesus Christ alone. They know that God's Word in Jesus Christ pronounces them guilty, even when they feel nothing of their own guilt, and that God's Word in Jesus Christ pronounces them free and righteous, even when they feel nothing of their own righteousness. Christians no longer live by their own resources, by accusing themselves and justifying themselves, but by God's accusation and God's justification. They live entirely by God's Word pronounced on them, in faithful submission to God's judgment, whether it declares them guilty or righteous. The death and life of Christians are not situated in a self-contained isolation. Rather, Christians encounter both death and life only in the Word that comes to them from the outside, in God's Word to them. The Reformers expressed it by calling our righteousness an "alien righteousness" ["fremde Gerechtigkeit"], a righteousness that comes from outside of us (*extra nos*). They meant by this expression that Christians are dependent on the Word of God spoken to them. They are directed outward to the Word coming to them. Christians live entirely by the truth of God's Word in Jesus Christ. If they are asked "where is your salvation, your blessedness, your righteousness?," they can never point to themselves. Instead,

5

they point to the Word of God in Jesus Christ that grants them salvation, blessedness, and righteousness. They watch for this Word wherever they can. Because they daily hunger and thirst for righteousness, they long for the redeeming Word again and again. It can only come from the outside. In themselves they are destitute and dead. Help must come from the outside; and it has come and comes daily and anew in the Word of Jesus Christ, bringing us redemption, righteousness, innocence, and blessedness. But God put this Word into the mouth of human beings so that it may be passed on to others. When people are deeply affected by the Word, they tell it to other people. God has willed that we should seek and find God's living Word in the testimony of other Christians, in the mouths of human beings. Therefore, Christians need other Christians who speak God's Word to them. They need them again and again when they become uncertain and disheartened because, living by their own resources, they cannot help themselves without cheating themselves out of the truth. They need other Christians as bearers and proclaimers of the divine word of salvation. They need them solely for the sake of Jesus Christ. The Christ in one's own heart is weaker than the Christ in the word of another Christian. The heart in one's heart is uncertain; the Word is sure. At the same time, this also clarifies that the goal of all Christian community is to encounter one another as bringers of the message of salvation. As such, God allows Christians to come together and grants them community. Their community is based only on Jesus Christ and this "alien righteousness." Therefore, we may now say that the community of Christians springs solely from the biblical and reformation message of the justification of human beings through grace alone. The longing of Christians for one another is based solely on this message.

Second, a Christian comes to others only through Jesus Christ. Among human beings there is strife. "He is our peace" (Eph. 2:14),

This is "holy Church?" cannot do "church" alone.

says Paul of Jesus Christ. In him, broken and divided humanity has become one. Without Christ there is discord between God and humanity and between one human being and another. Christ has become the mediator who has made peace with God and peace among human beings. Without Christ we would not know God; we could neither call on God nor come to God. Moreover, without Christ we would not know other Christians around us; nor could we approach them. The way to them is blocked by one's own ego [das eigene Ich]. Christ opened up the way to God and to one another. Now Christians can live with each other in peace; they can love and serve one another; they can become one. But they can continue to do so only through Jesus Christ. Only in Jesus Christ are we one; only through him are we bound together. He remains the one and only mediator throughout eternity.

Third, when God's Son took on flesh, he truly and bodily, out of pure grace, took on our being, our nature, ourselves. This was the eternal decree of the triune God. Now we are in him. Wherever he is, he bears our flesh, he bears us. And, where he is, there we are too—in the incarnation, on the cross, and in his resurrection. We belong to him because we are in him. That is why the Scriptures call us the body of Christ. But if we have been elected and accepted with the whole church in Jesus Christ before we could know it or want it, then we also belong to Christ in eternity with one another. We who live here in community with Christ will one day be with Christ in eternal community. Those who look at other Christians should know that they will be eternally united with them in Jesus Christ. Christian community means community through and in Jesus Christ. Everything the Scriptures provide in the way of directions and rules for Christians' life together rests on this presupposition.

"Now concerning love of the brothers and sisters, you do not need to have anyone write to you, for you yourselves have been taught by God to love one another. . . .But we urge you, beloved, to do so more and more" (1 Thess. 4:9f.). It is God's own undertaking to teach such love. All that human beings can add is to remember this divine instruction and the exhortation to excel in it more and more. When God had mercy on us, when God revealed Jesus Christ to us as our brother, when God won our hearts by God's own love, our instruction in Christian love began at the same time. When God was merciful to us, we learned to be merciful with one another. When we received forgiveness instead of judgment, we too were made ready to forgive each other. What God did to us, we then owed to others. The more we received, the more we were able to give; and the more meager our love for one another, the less we were living by God's mercy and love. Thus God taught us to encounter one another as God has encountered us in Christ. "Welcome one another, therefore, just as Christ has welcomed you, for the glory of God" (Rom. 15:7).

In this way the one whom God has placed in common life with other Christians learns what it means to have brothers and sisters. "Brothers and sisters . . . in the Lord," Paul calls his congregation (Phil. 1:14). One is a brother or sister to another only through Jesus Christ. I am a brother or sister to another person through what Jesus Christ has done for me and to me; others have become brothers and sisters to me through what Jesus Christ has done for them and to them. The fact that we are brothers and sisters only through Jesus Christ is of immeasurable significance. Therefore, the other who comes face to face with me earnestly and devoutly seeking community is not the brother or sister with whom I am to relate in the community. My brother or sister is instead that other person who has been redeemed by Christ, absolved from sin, and called to faith and eternal life. What persons are in themselves as Christians, in their inwardness and piety, cannot constitute the basis of our community, which is determined by what those persons are in terms of Christ.

Our community consists solely in what Christ has done to both of us. That not only is true at the beginning, as if in the course of time something else were to be added to our community, but also remains so for all the future and into all eternity. I have community with others and will continue to have it only through Jesus Christ. The more genuine and the deeper our community becomes, the more everything else between us will recede, and the more clearly and purely will Jesus Christ and his work become the one and only thing that is alive between us. We have one another only through Christ, but through Christ we really do *have* one another. We have one another completely and for all eternity.

This dismisses at the outset every unhappy desire for something more. Those who want more than what Christ has established between us do not want Christian community. They are looking for some extraordinary experiences of community that were denied them elsewhere. Such people are bringing confused and tainted desires into the Christian community. Precisely at this point Christian community is most often threatened from the very outset by the greatest danger, the danger of internal poisoning, the danger of confusing Christian community with some wishful image of pious community, the danger of blending the devout heart's natural desire for community with the spiritual reality of Christian community. It is essential for Christian community that two things become clear right from the beginning. *First, Christian community is not an ideal, but a divine reality; second, Christian community is a spiritual [pneumatisch] and not an emotional [psychisch] reality.*

On innumerable occasions a whole Christian community has been shattered because it has lived on the basis of a wishful image. Certainly serious Christians who are put in a community for the first time will often bring with them a very definite image of what Christian communal life [Zusammenleben] should be, and they will be anxious to realize it. But God's grace quickly frustrates all such dreams. A great disillusionment with others, with Christians in general, and, if we are fortunate, with ourselves, is bound to overwhelm us as surely as God desires to lead us to an understanding of genuine Christian community. By sheer grace God will not permit us to live in a dream world even for a few weeks and to abandon ourselves to those blissful experiences and exalted moods that sweep over us like a wave of rapture. For God is not a God of emotionalism, but the God of truth. Only that community which enters into the experience of this great disillusionment with all its unpleasant and evil appearances begins to be what it should be in God's sight, begins to grasp in faith the promise that is given to it. The sooner this moment of disillusionment comes over the individual and the community, the better for both. However, a community that cannot bear and cannot survive such disillusionment, clinging instead to its idealized image, when that should be done away with, loses at the same time the promise of a durable Christian community. Sooner or later it is bound to collapse. Every human idealized image that is brought into the Christian community is a hindrance to genuine community and must be broken up so that genuine community can survive. Those who love their dream of a Christian community more than the Christian community itself become destroyers of that Christian community even though their personal intentions may be ever so honest, earnest, and sacrificial.

God hates this wishful dreaming because it makes the dreamer proud and pretentious. Those who dream of this idealized community demand that it be fulfilled by God, by others, and by themselves. They enter the community of Christians with their demands, set up their own law, and judge one another and even God accordingly. They stand adamant, a living reproach to all others in the circle of the community. They act as if they have to create

→ all will not be goodness + light — much forgiveness needed. People only perfect in Christ

the Christian community, as if their visionary ideal binds the people together. Whatever does not go their way, they call a failure. When their idealized image is shattered, they see the community breaking into pieces. So they first become accusers of other Christians in the community, then accusers of God, and finally the desperate accusers of themselves. Because God already has laid the only foundation of our community, because God has united us in one body with other Christians in Jesus Christ long before we entered into common life with them, we enter into that life together with other Christians, not as those who make demands, but as those who thankfully receive. We thank God for what God has done for us. We thank God for giving us other Christians who live by God's call, forgiveness, and promise. We do not complain about what God does not give us; rather we are thankful for what God does give us daily. And is not what has been given us enough: other believers who will go on living with us through sin and need under the blessing of God's grace? Is the gift of God any less immeasurably great than this on any given day, even on the most difficult and distressing days of a Christian community? Even when sin and misunderstanding burden the common life, is not the one who sins still a person with whom I too stand under the word of Christ? Will not another Christian's sin be an occasion for me ever anew to give thanks that both of us may live in the forgiving love of God in Jesus Christ? Therefore, will not the very moment of great disillusionment with my brother or sister be incomparably wholesome for me because it so thoroughly teaches me that both of us can never live by our own words and deeds, but only by that one Word and deed that really binds us together, the forgiveness of sins in Jesus Christ? The bright day of Christian community dawns wherever the early morning mists of dreamy visions are lifting.

Thankfulness works in the Christian community as it usually does in the Christian life. Only those who give thanks for little things

> How large is "Community"? Is it the Church or the world?

11

receive the great things as well. We prevent God from giving us the great spiritual gifts prepared for us because we do not give thanks for daily gifts. We think that we should not be satisfied with the small measure of spiritual knowledge, experience, and love that has been given to us, and that we must be constantly seeking the great gifts. Then we complain that we lack the deep certainty, the strong faith, and the rich experiences that God has given to other Christians, and we consider these complaints to be pious. We pray for the big things and forget to give thanks for the small (and yet really not so small!) gifts we receive daily. How can God entrust great things to those who will not gratefully receive the little things from God's hand? If we do not give thanks daily for the Christian community in which we have been placed, even when there are no great experiences, no noticeable riches, but much weakness, difficulty, and little faith—and if, on the contrary, we only keep complaining to God that everything is so miserable and so insignificant and does not at all live up to our expectations—then we hinder God from letting our community grow according to the measure and riches that are there for us all in Jesus Christ. That also applies in a special way to the complaints often heard from pastors and zealous parishioners about their congregations. Pastors should not complain about their congregation, certainly never to other people, but also not to God. Congregations have not been entrusted to them in order that they should become accusers of their congregations before God and their fellow human beings. When pastors lose faith in a Christian community in which they have been placed and begin to make accusations against it, they had better examine themselves first to see whether the underlying problem is not their own idealized image, which should be shattered by God. And if they find that to be true, let them thank God for leading them into this predicament. But if they find that it is not true, let them nevertheless guard against ever becoming an accuser of those whom God has gathered together. Instead, let them accuse themselves of their unbelief, let them ask for an understanding of their own failure and their particular sin, and pray that they may not wrong other Christians. Let such pastors, recognizing their own guilt, make intercession for those charged to their care. Let them do what they have been instructed to do and thank God.

Like the Christian's sanctification, Christian community is a gift of God to which we have no claim. Only God knows the real condition of either our community or our sanctification. What may appear weak and insignificant to us may be great and glorious to God. Just as Christians should not be constantly feeling the pulse of their spiritual life, so too the Christian community has not been given to us by God for us to be continually taking its temperature. The more thankfully we daily receive what is given to us, the more assuredly and consistently will community increase and grow from day to day as God pleases.

Christian community is not an ideal we have to realize, but rather a reality created by God in Christ in which we may participate. The more clearly we learn to recognize that the ground and strength and promise of all our community is in Jesus Christ alone, the more calmly we will learn to think about our community and pray and hope for it.

Because Christian community is founded solely on Jesus Christ, it is a spiritual [pneumatisch] and not a emotional [psychisch] reality. In this respect it differs absolutely from all other communities. The Scriptures call pneumatic or "spiritual" [geistlich] what is created only by the Holy Spirit, who puts Jesus Christ into our hearts as lord and savior. The scriptures call "emotional" what comes from the natural urges, strengths, and abilities of the human soul.

The basis of all pneumatic, or spiritual, reality is the clear, manifest

Word of God in Jesus Christ. At the foundation of all emotional, reality are the dark, impenetrable urges and desires of the human soul. The basis of spiritual community is truth; the basis of emotional community is desire. The essence of spiritual community is light. For "God is light and in [God] there is no darkness at all" (1 John 1:5); and "if we walk in the light as he himself is in the light, we have fellowship with one another" (1 John 1:7). The essence of emotional community is darkness, "for it is from within, from the human heart, that evil intentions come" (Mark 7:21). It is the deep night that spreads over the sources of all human activity, over even all noble and devout impulses. Spiritual community is the community of those who are called by Christ; emotional community is the community of pious [fromm] souls. The bright love of Christian service, *agape*, lives in the spiritual community; the dark love of pious-impious urges, *eros*, burns in the emotional community. In the former, there is ordered, Christian service; in the latter, disordered desire for pleasure. In the former, there is humble submission of Christians one to another; in the latter, humble yet haughty subjection of other Christians to one's own desires. In the spiritual community the Word of God alone rules; in the emotional community the individual who is equipped with exceptional powers, experience, and magical, suggestive abilities rules along with the Word. In the one, God's Word alone is binding; in the other, besides the Word, human beings bind others to themselves. In the one, all power, honor, and rule are surrendered to the Holy Spirit; in the other, power and personal spheres of influence are sought and cultivated. So far as these are devout people, they certainly seek this power with the intention of serving the highest and the best. But in reality they end up dethroning the Holy Spirit and banishing it to the realm of unreal remoteness; only what is emotional remains real here. Thus, in the spiritual community the Spirit rules; in the emotional community, psychological techniques and methods. In the former, unsophisticated, nonpsychological, unmethodical, helping love is offered to one another; in the latter, psychological analysis and design. In the former, service to one another is simple and humble; in the latter, it is to strangers treated in a searching, calculating fashion.

Perhaps the contrast between spiritual and emotional reality can be made most clear in the following observation. Within the spiritual community there is never, in any way whatsoever, an "immediate" relationship of one to another. However, in the emotional community there exists a profound, elemental emotional desire for community, for immediate contact with other human souls, just as in the flesh there is a yearning for immediate union with other flesh. This desire of the human soul seeks the complete intimate fusion of I and You, whether this occurs in the union of love or—what from this emotional perspective is after all the same thing—in forcing the other into one's own sphere of power and influence. Here is where emotional, strong persons enjoy life to the full, securing for themselves the admiration, the love, or the fear of the weak. Here human bonds, suggestive influences, and dependencies are everything. Moreover, everything that is originally and solely characteristic of the community mediated through Christ reappears in the nonmediated community of souls in a distorted form.

There is, likewise, such a thing as "emotional" conversion. It has all the appearances of genuine conversion and occurs wherever the superior power of one person is consciously or unconsciously misused to shake to the roots and draw into its spell an individual or a whole community. Here one soul has had an immediate effect on another. The result is that the weak individual has been overcome by the strong; the resistance of the weaker individual has broken down under the influence of the other person. One has been overpowered by something, but not won over. This becomes apparent the moment

Interesting distinction.

a commitment is demanded, a commitment that must be made independently of the person to whom one is bound or possibly in opposition to this person. Here is where those emotional converts fail. They thus show that their conversion was brought about not by the Holy Spirit, but by a human being. It is, therefore, not enduring.

There is, likewise, a "merely emotional" love of neighbor. Such love is capable of making the most unheard-of sacrifices. Often it far surpasses the genuine love of Christ in fervent devotion and visible results. It speaks the Christian language with overwhelming and stirring eloquence. But it is what the apostle Paul is speaking of when he says: "If I give all I possess to the poor, and surrender my body to the flames" (1 Cor. 13:3)—in other words, if I combine the utmost deeds of love with the utmost of devotion—"but do not have love (that is, the love of Christ), I would be nothing" (1 Cor. 13:2). Emotional love loves the other for the sake of itself; spiritual love loves the other for the sake of Christ. That is why emotional love seeks direct contact with other persons. It loves them, not as free persons, but as those whom it binds to itself. It wants to do everything it can to win and conquer; it puts pressure on the other person. It desires to be irresistible, to dominate. Emotional love does not think much of truth. It makes the truth relative, since nothing, not even the truth, must come between it and the person loved. Emotional love desires other persons, their company. It wants them to return its love, but it does not serve them. On the contrary, it continues to desire even when it seems to be serving.

Two factors, which are really one and the same thing, reveal the difference between spiritual and emotional love. Emotional love cannot tolerate the dissolution of a community that has become false, even for the sake of genuine community. And such emotional love cannot love an enemy, that is to say, one who seriously and stubbornly resists it. Both spring from the same source: emotional love is by its very nature desire, desire for emotional community. As long as it can possibly satisfy this desire, it will not give it up, even for the sake of truth, even for the sake of genuine love for others. But emotional love is at an end when it can no longer expect its desire to be fulfilled, namely, in the face of an enemy. There it turns into hatred, contempt, and slander.

Spiritual love, however, begins right at this point. This is why emotional love turns into personal hatred when it encounters genuine spiritual love that does not desire but serves. Emotional love makes itself an end in itself. It turns itself into an achievement, an idol it worships, to which it must subject everything. It cares for, cultivates, and loves itself and nothing else in the world. Spiritual love, however, comes from Jesus Christ; it serves him alone. It knows that it has no direct access to other persons. Christ stands between me and others. I do not know in advance what love of others means on the basis of the general idea of love that grows out of my emotional desires. All this may instead be hatred and the worst kind of selfishness in the eyes of Christ. Only Christ in his Word tells me what love is. Contrary to all my own opinions and convictions, Jesus Christ will tell me what love for my brothers and sisters really looks like. Therefore, spiritual love is bound to the word of Jesus Christ alone. Where Christ tells me to maintain community for the sake of love, I desire to maintain it. Where the truth of Christ orders me to dissolve a community for the sake of love, I will dissolve it, despite all the protests of my emotional love. Because spiritual love does not desire but rather serves, it loves an enemy as a brother or sister. It originates neither in the brother or sister nor in the enemy, but in Christ and his word. Emotional love can never comprehend spiritual love, for spiritual love is from above. It is something completely strange, new, and incomprehensible to all earthly love.

Because Christ stands between me and an other, I must not long for unmediated community with that person. As only Christ was able to speak to me in such a way that I was helped, so others too can only be helped by Christ alone. However, this means that I must release others from all my attempts to control, coerce, and dominate them with my love. In their freedom from me, other persons want to be loved for who they are, as those for whom Christ became a human being, died, and rose again, as those for whom Christ won the forgiveness of sins and prepared eternal life. Because Christ has long since acted decisively for other Christians, before I could begin to act, I must allow them the freedom to be Christ's. They should encounter me only as the persons that they already are for Christ. This is the meaning of the claim that we can encounter others only through the mediation of Christ. Emotional love constructs its own image of other persons, about what they are and what they should become. It takes the life of the other person into its own hands. Spiritual love recognizes the true image of the other person as seen from the perspective of Jesus Christ. It is the image Jesus Christ has formed and wants to form in all people.

Therefore, spiritual love will prove successful insofar as it commends the other to Christ in all that it says and does. It will not seek to agitate another by exerting all too personal, direct influence or by crudely interfering in one's life. It will not take pleasure in pious, emotional fervor and excitement. Rather, it will encounter the other with the clear word of God and be prepared to leave the other alone with this word for a long time. It will be willing to release others again so that Christ may deal with them. It will respect the boundary of the other, which is placed between us by Christ, and it will find full community with the other in the Christ who alone binds us together. This spiritual love will thus speak to Christ about the other Christian more than to the other Christian about Christ. It knows that the most direct way to others is always through prayer to Christ and that love of the other is completely tied to the truth found in Christ. It is out of this love that John the disciple speaks: "I have no greater joy than this, to hear that my children are walking in the truth" (3 John 4).

Emotional love lives by uncontrolled and uncontrollable dark desires; spiritual love lives in the clear light of service ordered by the *truth*. Emotional love results in human enslavement, bondage, rigidity; spiritual love creates the *freedom* of Christians under the Word. Emotional love breeds artificial hothouse flowers; spiritual love creates the *fruits* that grow healthily under God's open sky, according to God's good pleasure in the rain and storm and sunshine.

Good metaphor

The existence of any Christian communal life essentially depends on whether or not it succeeds at the right time in promoting the ability to distinguish between a human ideal and God's reality, between spiritual and emotional community. The life and death of a Christian community is decided by its ability to reach sober clarity on these points as soon as possible. In other words, a life together under the Word will stay healthy only when it does not form itself into a movement, an order, a society, a *collegium pietatis*, but instead understands itself as being part of the one, holy, universal, Christian church, sharing through its deeds and suffering in the hardships and struggles and promise of the whole church. Every principle of selection, and every division connected with it that is not necessitated quite objectively by common work, local conditions, or family connections is of the greatest danger to a Christian community. Self-centeredness always insinuates itself in any process of intellectual or spiritual selectivity, destroying the spiritual power of the community and robbing the community of its effectiveness for the church, thus driving it into sectarianism. The exclusion of the weak and insignificant, the seemingly useless people, from everyday Christian life in community [Lebensgemeinschaft] may actually mean the exclusion of Christ; for in the poor sister or brother, Christ is knocking at the door. We must, therefore, be very careful on this point.

The undiscerning observer may think that this mixture of ideal and real, emotional and spiritual, would be most obvious where there are a number of layers in the structure of a community, as in marriage, the family, friendship—where the emotional element as such already assumes a central importance in the community's coming into being at all, and where the spiritual is only something added to humanity's physical-emotional [leiblich-seelischen] nature. According to this view, it is only in these multifaceted communities that there is a danger of confusing and mixing the two spheres, whereas such a danger could hardly arise in a community of a purely spiritual nature. Such ideas, however, are a grand delusion. On the basis of all our experience—and as can be easily seen from the very nature of things—the truth is just the opposite. A marriage, a family, a friendship knows exactly the limitations of its community-building power. Such relationships know very well, if they are sound, where the emotional element ends and the spiritual begins. They are aware of the difference between physical-emotional and spiritual community. On the other hand, whenever a community of a purely spiritual nature comes together, the danger is uncannily near that everything pertaining to emotion will be brought into and intermixed with this community. Purely spiritual life in community [Lebensgemeinschaft] is not only dangerous but also not normal. Whenever physical-familial community, the community formed among those engaged in serious work, or everyday life with all its demands on working people is not introduced into the spiritual community, extraordinary vigilance and clear thinking are called for. That is why it is precisely on short retreats that, as experience has shown, emotion spreads most easily. Nothing is easier than to stimulate the euphoria of community in a few days of life together [gemeinsame Leben]; and nothing is more fatal to the healthy, sober, everyday life in community of Christians.

There is probably no Christian to whom God has not given the uplifting and blissful *experience* of genuine Christian community at least once in her or his life. But in this world such experiences remain nothing but a gracious extra beyond the daily bread of Christian community life. We have no claim to such experiences, and we do not live with other Christians for the sake of gaining such experiences. It is not the experience of Christian community, but firm and certain faith within Christian community that holds us together. We hold fast in faith to God's greatest gift, that God has acted for us all and wants to act for us all. This makes us joyful and happy, but it also makes us ready to forgo all such experiences if at times God does not grant them. We are bound together by faith, not by experience.

"How very good and pleasant it is when kindred live together in unity." This is the Scripture's praise of life together under the Word. But now we can correctly interpret the words "in unity" and say "when kindred live together through Christ." For Jesus Christ alone is our unity. "He is our peace." We have access to one another, joy in one another, community with one another through Christ alone.

Emotional - Spiritual Love

Together See other
Through Christ
[illegible] Love for [illegible]

Church/Body of Christ/Other people
1. Grace alone
2. Come to others through Christ
3. We are the Body, the incarnation – But elect
Emotional v. Spiritual Community –
Listening v. Preaching

Because we are in Christ, the body of God/community already exists, is real – we participate in it (or not?)

The Day Together

To you our morning song of praise,
To you our evening prayer we raise;
In lowly song your glory we adore
O God, now, forever and forevermore.
(Luther, following Ambrose)

"Let the word of Christ dwell in you richly" (Col. 3:16). The Old Testament day begins on one evening and ends with the sundown of the next evening. That is the time of expectation. The day of the New Testament church begins at sunrise in the early morning and ends with the dawning light of the next morning. That is the time of fulfillment, the resurrection of the Lord. At night Christ was born, a light in the darkness; noonday turned to night when Christ suffered and died on the cross. But early on Easter morning Christ emerged victorious from the grave. "Ere yet the dawn has filled the skies / Behold my Savior Christ arise, / He chases from us sin and night, / And brings us joy and life and light. Halleluia" So sang the church of the Reformation. Christ is the "Sun of righteousness," who has risen upon the expectant congregation (Mal. 4:2), and they who love him will be like the sun when it rises in its strength (Judg. 5:31). The early morning belongs to the church of the risen Christ. At the break of light it remembers the morning on which death, the devil, and sin were brought low in defeat, and new life and salvation were given to human beings.

What do we, who today no longer have any fear or awe of the darkness or night, know about the great joy that our forebears and the early Christians felt every morning at the return of the light? If we were to learn again something of the praise and adoration that is due the triune God early in the morning, then we would also begin to sense something of the joy that comes when night is past and those who dwell with one another come together early in the morning to praise their God and hear the Word and pray together. We would learn again of God the Father and Creator who has preserved our life through the dark night and awakened us to a new day; God the Son and Savior of the World, who vanquished death and hell for us, and dwells in our midst as Victor; God the Holy Spirit who pours the bright light of God's Word into our hearts early in the morning, driving away all darkness and sin and teaching us to pray the right way. Morning does not belong to the individual; it belongs to all the church of the triune God, to the community of Christians living together [Hausgemeinschaft], to the community of brothers [Bruderschaft]. The ancient hymns that call the community of faith to praise God together in the early morning are inexhaustible. That is why the Bohemian Brethren sing in this manner at the break of day: "The day does now dark night dispel; / Dear Christians, wake and rouse you well. / Your praises to the Lord sing true; / And pondering the image of God in you, / Proclaim the Lord's wonders ever anew. / Once more the daylight shines abroad, / O brethren, let us praise the Lord, / Whose grace and mercy thus have kept / The nightly watch while we have slept. / We beg your care this new born day, / For us, poor pilgrims on our way, / O by us stand to help and guide, / That evil on us ne'er betide. / For this there comes the light of day, / O brethren, let us thanksgiving say, / To gentle God who guarded us this darkened night, / Whose grace stood watch o'er us in every plight. / We offer up ourselves to you, / may our wants, words, and deeds be true. / In union with your heart will you us lead. / In you will our work be graced indeed."

Life together under the Word begins at an early hour of the day with a worship service together. A community living together gathers for praise and thanks, Scripture reading, and prayer. The profound silence of morning is first broken by the prayer and song of the community of faith. After the silence of the night and early morning, hymns and the Word of God will be heard all the more clearly. Along these lines the Holy Scriptures tell us that the first thought and the first word of the day belong to God: "O Lord, in the morning you hear my voice; in the morning I plead my case to you, and watch" (Ps. 5:4 [3]). "In the morning my prayer comes before you" (Ps. 88:14 [13]). "My heart is steadfast, O God, my heart is steadfast; I will sing and make melody. Awake, my soul! Awake, O harp and lyre! I will awake the dawn" (Ps. 57:8f. [7f.]). At the break of dawn the believer thirsts and yearns for God: "I rise before dawn and cry for help. I put my hope in your words" (Ps. 119:147). "O God, you are my God, I seek you, my soul thirsts for you; my flesh faints for you, as in a dry and weary land where there is no water" (Ps. 63:2 [1]). The Wisdom of Solomon would have it "known that one must rise before the sun to give you thanks, and must pray to you at the dawning of the light" (16:28), and Jesus Ben Sirach says especially of the teacher of the law that "he sets his heart to rise early to seek the Lord who made him, and to petition the Most High" (39:6 [5]). The Holy Scriptures also speak of the morning hours as the time of God's special help. It is said of the city of God: "God will help it when the morning dawns" (Ps. 46:6 [5]), and again, that God's blessings "are new every morning" (Lam. 3:23).

For Christians the beginning of the day should not be burdened and haunted by the various kinds of concerns they face during the working day. The Lord stands above the new day, for God has made it. All the darkness and confusion of the night with its dreams gives way to the clear light of Jesus Christ and his awakening Word. All restlessness, all impurity, all worry and anxiety flee before him. Therefore, in the early morning hours of the day may our many thoughts and our many idle words be silent, and may the first thought and the first word belong to the one to whom our whole life belongs. "Sleeper, awake! Rise from the dead, and Christ will shine on you" (Eph. 5:14).

With remarkable frequency the Holy Scriptures remind us of various men of God who got up early to seek God and carry out God's commands, as for example, Abraham, Jacob, Moses, and Joshua (cf. Gen. 19:27, 22:3; Exod. 8:16 [20], 9:13, 24:4; Josh. 3:1, 6:12, etc.). The Gospel, which never speaks a superfluous word, reports about Jesus himself: "In the morning, while it was still very dark, he got up and went out to a deserted place, and there he prayed" (Mark 1:35). Some people get up early because of uneasiness and worry; the Scriptures call that pointless, saying, "It is in vain that you rise up early . . . eating your bread with tears" (Ps. 127:2). But there is such a thing as rising early for the love of God. That was the practice of the men of the Holy Scriptures.

Scripture reading, song, and prayer should be part of daily morning *worship together* [gemeinsame Andacht]. Daily morning worship will take as many different forms as there are communities. That is the way it is bound to be. When a community living together includes children, it needs a different sort of daily worship than a community of seminarians. It is by no means healthy when one becomes like the other, when, for example, a brotherhood of seminarians is content with a form of family daily worship for children. However, the *word of Scripture, the hymns of the church, and the prayer of the community* should form a part of every daily worship that they share together. I will now speak here of the individual parts of such daily worship together.

"Speak to one another with psalms" (Eph. 5:19). "Teach and admonish one another . . . and . . . sing psalms" (Col. 3:16). From ancient times in the church a special significance has been attached to the *praying of Psalms* together. In many churches to this day the Psalter is used at the beginning of every service of daily worship together. The practice has been lost to a large extent, and we must now recover the meaning of praying the Psalms. The Psalter occupies a unique place in all the Holy Scriptures. It is God's Word, and with few exceptions it is at the same time the prayer of human beings. How are we to understand this? How can God's Word be at the same time prayer to God? This question is followed by an observation made by all who begin to pray the Psalms. First, they try to repeat the Psalms personally as their own prayer. But soon they come across passages that they feel they cannot pray as their own personal prayers. We remember, for example, the psalms of innocence, the psalms of vengeance, and also, in part, the psalms of suffering. Nevertheless, these prayers are words of the Holy Scriptures that believing Christians cannot simply dismiss as obsolete and antiquated, as a "preliminary stage of religion" ["religiöse Vorstufe"]. Thus they do not desire to gain control over the word of Scripture, and yet they realize that they cannot pray these words. They can read and hear them as the prayer of another person, wonder about them, be offended by them, but they can neither pray them themselves nor expunge them from the Holy Scriptures. The practical thing to say here would be that people in this situation should first stick to the psalms they can understand and pray, and that in reading the other psalms they should quite simply learn to overlook what is incomprehensible and difficult in the Holy Scriptures, returning again and again to what is simple and understandable. However, this difficulty actually indicates the point at which we may get our first glimpse of the secret of the Psalter. The psalms that will not cross our lips as prayers, those that make us falter and offend us, make us suspect that here someone else is praying, not we—that the one who is here affirming his innocence, who is calling for God's judgment, who has come to such infinite depths of suffering, is none other than Jesus Christ himself. It is he who is praying here, and not only here, but in the whole Psalter. The New Testament and the church have always recognized and testified to this truth. The *human* Jesus Christ to whom no affliction, no illness, no suffering is unknown, and who yet was the wholly innocent and righteous one, is praying in the Psalter through the mouth of his congregation. The Psalter is the prayer book of Jesus Christ in the truest sense of the word. He prayed the Psalter, and now it has become his prayer for all time. Can we now comprehend how the Psalter is capable of being simultaneously prayer to God and yet God's own Word, precisely because the praying Christ encounters us here? Jesus Christ prays the Psalter in his congregation. His congregation prays too, and even the individual prays. But they pray only insofar as Christ prays within them; they pray here not in their own name, but in the name of Jesus Christ. They pray not from the natural desires of their own hearts, but rather out of the humanity assumed by Christ. They pray on the basis of the prayer of the human Jesus Christ. Their prayer will be met with the promise of being heard only when they pray on this basis. Because Christ prays the prayer of the Psalms with the individual and with the church before the heavenly throne of God, or rather, because those who pray the Psalms are joining in the prayer of Jesus Christ, their prayer reaches the ears of God. Christ has become their intercessor.

The Psalter is the vicarious prayer of Christ for his congregation.

Now that Christ is with the Father, the new humanity of Christ—the body of Christ—on earth continues to pray his prayer to the end of time. This prayer belongs not to the individual member, but to the whole body of Christ. All the things of which the Psalter speaks, which individuals can never fully comprehend and call their own, live only in the body of Christ as a whole. That is why the prayer of the Psalms belongs in the community in a special way. Even if a verse or a psalm is not my own prayer, it is nevertheless the prayer of another member of the community; and it is quite certainly the prayer of the truly human Jesus Christ and his body on earth.

In the Psalter we learn to pray on the basis of Christ's prayer. The Psalter is the great school of prayer. *First*, we learn here what prayer means: it means praying on the basis of the Word of God, on the basis of promises. Christian prayer takes its stand on the solid ground of the revealed Word and has nothing to do with vague, self-seeking desires. We pray on the basis of the prayer of the truly human Jesus Christ. This is what the Scripture means when it says that the Holy Spirit prays in us and for us, that Christ prays for us, that we can pray to God in the right way only in the name of Jesus Christ.

Second, we learn from the prayer of the Psalms what we should pray. As certain as it is that the prayer of the Psalms ranges far beyond the experiences of the individual, nevertheless, the individual prays in faith the whole prayer of Christ, the prayer of one who was truly human and who alone possesses the full range of experiences expressed in these prayers. Can we, then, pray the psalms of vengeance? Insofar as we are sinners and associate evil thoughts with the prayer of vengeance, we must not do so. But insofar as Christ is in us, we, too, as members of Jesus Christ, can pray these psalms through and from the heart of Jesus Christ, who took all the vengeance of God on himself, who was afflicted in place of us by the vengeance of God, who was in this way stricken by the wrath of God and in no other way could forgive his enemies, and who himself suffered this wrath so that his enemies might go free. Can we, with the psalmist, call ourselves innocent, devout, and righteous? We cannot do so insofar as we are ourselves. We cannot do it as the prayer of our own perverse heart. But we can and should do it as a prayer from the heart of Jesus Christ that was sinless and pure, from the innocence of Christ in which he has given us a share by faith. Insofar as "Christ's blood and righteousness" have become "our robe of honor and adornment," we can and we should pray the psalms of innocence as Christ's prayer for us and gift to us. These psalms, too, belong to us through Christ. And how should we pray those prayers of unspeakable misery and suffering, since we have hardly begun to sense even remotely something of what is meant here? We can and we should pray the psalms of suffering, not to become completely caught up in something our heart does not know from its own experience, nor to make our own complaints, but because all this suffering was genuine and real in Jesus Christ, because the human being Jesus Christ suffered sickness, pain, shame, and death, and because in his suffering and dying all flesh suffered and died. What happened to us on the cross of Christ, the death of our old self, and what actually does happen and should happen to us since our baptism in the dying of our flesh, is what gives us the right to pray these prayers. Through the cross of Jesus these psalms have been granted to his body on earth as prayers that issue from his heart. We cannot elaborate on this theme here. Our concern has been only to suggest the depth and breadth of the Psalter as the prayer of Christ. In this regard, we can only grow into the Psalter gradually.

Third, the prayer of the Psalms teaches us to pray as a community. The body of Christ is praying, and I as an individual recognize that my prayer is only a tiny fraction of the whole prayer of the church. I learn to join the body of Christ in its prayer. That lifts me above my personal concerns and allows me to pray selflessly. Many of the Psalms were very probably prayed antiphonally by the Old Testament congregation. The so-called parallelism of the verses (*parallelismus membrorum*), that remarkable repetition of the same idea in different words in the second line of the verse, is not merely a literary form. It also has meaning for the church and theology. It would be worthwhile sometime to pursue this question very thoroughly. One might read, as a particularly clear example, Psalm 5. Repeatedly there are two voices, bringing the same prayer request to God in different words. Is that not meant to be an indication that the one who prays never prays alone? There must always be a second person, another, a member of the church, the body of Christ, indeed Jesus Christ himself, praying with the Christian in order that the prayer of the individual may be true prayer. In the repetition of the same subject, which is heightened in Psalm 119 to such a degree that it seems it does not want to end and becomes so simple that it is virtually impervious to our exegetical analysis, is there not the suggestion that every word of prayer must penetrate to a depth of the heart which can be reached only by unceasing repetition? And in the end not even in that way! Is that not an indication that prayer is not a matter of a unique pouring out of the human heart in need or joy, but an unbroken, indeed continuous, process of learning, appropriating and impressing God's will in Jesus Christ on the mind? Ötinger, in his exegesis of the Psalms, brought out a profound truth when he arranged the whole Psalter according to the seven petitions of the Lord's Prayer. What he meant was that the long and extensive book of Psalms was concerned with nothing more or less than the brief petitions of the Lord's Prayer. In all our praying there remains only the prayer of Jesus Christ, which has the promise of fulfillment and frees us from the vain repetitions of the heathen. The more deeply we grow into the Psalms and the more often we ourselves have prayed them, the more simple and rewarding will our praying become.

The prayer of the Psalms, concluded with a hymn by the house church [Hausgemeinde], is followed by a *Scripture reading*. "Give attention to the public reading of scripture" (1 Tim. 4:13). Here, too, we will have to overcome some harmful prejudices before we achieve the right way of reading the Scripture together. Almost all of us have grown up with the idea that the Scripture reading is solely a matter of hearing the Word of God for today. That is why for many the Scripture reading consists only of a few brief selected verses that are to form the central idea of the day. There can be no doubt that the daily Bible passages published by the Moravian Brethren, for example, are a real blessing to all who have ever used them. Many people have realized that to their great amazement and have been grateful for the daily Bible readings particularly during the time of the church struggle [Kirchenkampf]. But equally there can be little doubt that brief passages cannot and must not take the place of reading the Scripture as a whole. The verse for the day is not yet the Holy Scriptures that will remain throughout all time until the Day of Judgment. The Holy Scriptures are more than selected Bible passages. It is also more than "Bread for Today." It is God's revealed Word for all peoples, for all times. The Holy Scriptures do not consist of individual sayings, but are a whole and can be used most effectively as such. The Scriptures are God's revealed Word as a whole. The full witness to Jesus Christ the Lord can be clearly heard only in its immeasurable inner relationships, in the connection of Old and New Testaments, of promise and fulfillment, sacrifice and law, Law and Gospel, cross and resurrection, faith and obedience, having and hoping. That is why daily worship together must include a longer Old and New Testament lesson besides the prayer of the Psalms. A community of Christians living together surely should be able to read and listen to a chapter of the Old Testament and at least half a chapter of the New Testament every morning and evening. When the practice is first tried, however, such a community will discover that even this modest measure represents a maximum demand for most people and will meet with resistance. It will be objected that it is impossible really to take in and retain such an abundance of ideas and interconnections, that it even shows disrespect for God's Word to read more than one can seriously digest. In the face of these objections, we will easily content ourselves again with reading only verses. In truth, however, a serious failing lies hidden beneath this attitude. If it is really true that it is hard for us, as adult Christians, to comprehend a chapter of the Old Testament in its context, then that can only fill us with profound shame. What kind of testimony is that to our knowledge of the Scriptures and all our previous reading of them? If we were familiar with the substance of what we read, we could follow the reading of a chapter without difficulty, especially if we have an open Bible in our hands and are reading it at the same time. However, since that is not the case, we must admit that the Holy Scriptures are still largely unknown to us. Can this sin of our own ignorance of God's Word have any other consequence than that we should earnestly and faithfully recover lost ground and catch up on what we have missed? And should not the seminarians be the very first to get to work here? Let us not argue that it is not the purpose of daily worship together to get to know the contents of Scripture, that this is too profane a purpose, something that must be achieved apart from daily worship. This argument is based on a completely wrong understanding of what a daily worship service is. God's Word is to be heard by all in their own way and according to the measure of their understanding. A child hears and learns the biblical story for the first time during daily worship. Mature Christians keep on learning it and learn it better and better; and as they read and hear it on their own, they will never finish this learning.

Not only immature Christians, but also mature Christians will complain that the Scripture reading is often too long for them and that there is much they do not grasp. In response to this complaint it must be said that indeed for the mature Christian every Scripture reading will be "too long," even the shortest one. What does that mean? The Scripture is a complex unity, and every word, every sentence, contains such a diversity of relationships to the whole that it is impossible always to keep track of the whole when listening to an individual portion of it. Therefore, it appears that the whole of Scripture as well as every passage in it far surpasses our understanding. It can only be a good thing when we are daily reminded of this fact, which again refers us to Jesus Christ himself "in whom are *hidden* all the treasures of wisdom and knowledge" (Col. 2:3). So one may perhaps say that every Scripture reading always has to be somewhat "too long" if it is not to be aphoristic worldly wisdom, but God's Word of revelation in Jesus Christ.

Because the Scripture is a corpus, a living whole, the so-called *lectio continua*, or consecutive reading, will above all be worth considering for the Scripture reading of the house church. Historical books, the Prophets, Gospels, Epistles, and Revelation are read and heard as God's Word in their context. They put the listening congregation in the midst of the wonderful revelatory world of the people of Israel with their prophets, judges, kings, and priests, with their wars, festivals, sacrifices, and sufferings. The community of believers is drawn into the Christmas story, the baptism, the miracles and discourses, the suffering, dying, and rising of Jesus Christ. It participates in the events that once occurred on this earth for the salvation of the whole world. In so doing, it receives salvation in Jesus Christ here and in all these events. For those who want to hear, reading the biblical books in a sequential order forces them to go, and to allow themselves to be found, where God has acted once and for all for the salvation of human beings. The historical books of the Holy Scriptures come alive for us in a whole new way precisely when they are read during worship services. We receive a part of that which once took place for our salvation. Forgetting and losing ourselves, we too pass through the Red Sea, through the desert, across the Jordan into the promised land. With Israel we fall into doubt and unbelief and through punishment and repentance experience again God's help and faithfulness. All this is not mere reverie, but holy, divine reality. We are uprooted from our own existence and are taken back to the holy history of God on earth. There God has dealt with us, and there God still deals with us today, with our needs and our sins, by means of the divine wrath and grace. What is important is not that God is a spectator and participant in our life today, but that we are attentive listeners and participants in God's action in the sacred story, the story of Christ on earth. God is with us today only as long as we are there. A complete reversal occurs here. It is not that God's help and presence must still be proved in our life; rather God's presence and help have been demonstrated for us in the life of Jesus Christ. It is in fact more important for us to know what God did to Israel, in God's son Jesus Christ, than to discover what God intends for us today. The fact that Jesus Christ died is more important than the fact that I will die. And the fact that Jesus Christ was raised from the dead is the sole ground of my hope that I, too, will be raised on the day of judgment. Our salvation is "from outside ourselves" (*extra nos*). I find salvation not in my life story, but only in the story of Jesus Christ. Only those who allow themselves to be found in Jesus Christ—in the incarnation, cross, and resurrection—are with God and God with them.

From this perspective the whole reading of the Holy Scriptures in worship services becomes every day more meaningful and more beneficial. What we call our life, our troubles, and our guilt is by no means the whole of reality; our life, our need, our guilt, and our deliverance are there in the Scriptures. Because it pleased God to act for us there, it is only there that we will be helped. Only in the Holy Scriptures do we get to know our own story. The God of Abraham, Isaac, and Jacob is the God and Father of Jesus Christ and our God.

We must once again get to know the Scriptures as the reformers and our forebears knew them. We must not shy away from the work and the time required for this task. We must become acquainted with the Scriptures first and foremost for the sake of our salvation. But, besides this, there are enough weighty reasons to make this challenge absolutely urgent for us. For example, how are we ever to gain certainty and confidence in our personal deeds and church activity if we do not stand on solid biblical ground? It is not our heart that determines our course, but God's Word. But who in this day has any proper awareness of the need for evidence from Scripture? How often do we hear innumerable arguments "from life" and "from experience" to justify the most crucial decisions? Yet the evidence of Scripture is excluded even though it would perhaps point in exactly the opposite direction. It is not surprising, of course, that those who attempt to discredit the evidence of Scripture are the people who themselves do not seriously read, know, or make a thorough study of the Scriptures. But those who are not willing to learn how to deal with the Scriptures for themselves are not Protestant Christians [evangelischer Christen].

Perhaps we should ask a further question: How are we supposed to help rightly other Christians who are experiencing troubles and temptation [Anfechtung] if not with God's own Word? All our own words quickly fail. However, those who "like the master of a household who brings out of his treasure what is new and what is old" (Matt. 13:52)—who can speak out of the abundance of God's Word the wealth of instructions, admonitions, and comforting words from the Scriptures—will be able to drive out demons and help one another through God's Word. We will stop here. "From childhood you have known the sacred writings that are able to instruct you for salvation" (2 Tim. 3:15).

How should we read the Holy Scriptures? In a community living together it is best that its various members assume the task of consecutive reading by taking turns. When this is done, the community will see that it is not easy to read the Scriptures aloud for others. The reading will better suit the subject matter the more plain and simple it is, the more focused it is on the subject matter, the more humble one's attitude. Often the difference between an experienced Christian and a beginner comes out clearly when Scripture is read aloud. It may be taken as a rule for the correct reading of Scripture that the readers should never identify themselves with the person who is speaking in the Bible. It is not I who am angry, but God; it is not I giving comfort, but God; it is not I admonishing, but God admonishing in the Scriptures. Of course, I will be able to express the fact that it is God who is angry, God who is giving comfort and admonishing, by speaking not in a detached, monotonous voice, but only with heartfelt involvement, as one who knows that I myself am being addressed. However, it will make all the difference between a right and a wrong way of reading Scripture if I do not confuse myself with, but rather quite simply serve, God. Otherwise I become rhetorical, over-emotional, sentimental, or coercive; that is to say, I divert the reader's attention to myself instead of the Word—this is the sin of Scripture reading. If we could illustrate this with an example from everyday life, the situation of the one who is reading the Scripture would probably come closest to that in which I read to another person a letter from a friend. I would not read the letter as though I had written it myself. The distance between us would be clearly noticeable as it was read. And yet I would also not be able to read my friend's letter as if it were of no concern to me. On the contrary, because of our close relationship, I would read it with personal interest. Proper reading of Scripture is not a technical exercise that can be learned; it is something that grows or diminishes according to my own spiritual condition. The ponderous, laborious reading of the Bible by many a Christian who has become seasoned through experience often far surpasses a minister's reading, no matter how perfect the latter in form. In a community of Christians living together, one person may also give counsel and help to another in this matter.

The short devotional Bible texts do not need to be lost but can supplement the continuous reading of the Scriptures. They may find their place as weekly or as daily Bible verses at the beginning of daily worship or at some other time.

Singing together [das gemeinsame Lied] joins the praying of the Psalms and the reading of the Scriptures. In this, the voice of the church is heard in praise, thanksgiving, and intercession.

"O sing to the Lord a new song," the Psalter calls out to us again and again. It is the Christ hymn, new every morning, that a community living together begins to sing in the early morning, the new song that is sung by the whole community of faith in God on earth and in heaven. We are called to join in the singing of it. It is God who has prepared one great song of praise throughout eternity, and those who enter God's community join in this song. It is the song that "the morning stars sang together and all the children of God shouted for joy" (Job 38:7). It is the victory song of the children of Israel after passing through the Red Sea, the Magnificat of Mary after the Annunciation, the song of Paul and Silas when they praised God in the darkness of prison, the song of the singers on the sea of glass after their deliverance, the "song of Moses, the servant of God, and the song of the Lamb" (Rev. 15:3). It is the new song of the heavenly community. Every day in the morning the community of faith on earth joins in this song and in the evening it closes the day with this hymn. The triune God and the works of God are being extolled here. This song has a different sound on earth than it does in heaven. On earth, it is the song of those who believe; in heaven, the song of those who see. On earth, it is a song expressed in inadequate human words; in heaven they are the "things that are not to be told, that no mortal is permitted to repeat" (2 Cor. 12:4), the "new song that no one could learn, except the 144,000" (Rev. 14:3), the song to which the "harps of God" are played (Rev. 15:2). What do we know of that new song and the harps of God? Our new song is an earthly song, a song of pilgrims and sojourners on whom the Word of God has dawned to light their way. Our earthly song is bound to God's Word of revelation in Jesus Christ. It is the simple song of the children of this earth who have been called to be God's children, not ecstatic, not enraptured, but soberly, gratefully, devoutly focused on God's revealed Word.

"Sing and make music in your heart to the Lord" (Eph. 5:19). The new song is sung first in the heart. It cannot be sung at all in any other way. The heart sings because it is filled with Christ. That is why all singing in the congregation is a spiritual thing. Devotion to the Word, incorporation into the community, great humility, and much discipline—these are the prerequisites of all singing together. Wherever the heart does not join in the singing, there is only the dreadful muddle of human self-praise. Wherever the singing is not to the Lord, it is singing to the honor of the self or the music, and the new song becomes a song to idols.

"Speak to one another with psalms, hymns and spiritual songs" (Eph. 5:19). Our song on earth is speech. It is the sung Word. Why do Christians sing when they are together? The reason is, quite simply, that in singing together it is possible for them to speak and pray the same Word at the same time—in other words, for the sake of uniting in the Word. All daily worship, all human concentration should be focused on the Word in the hymn. The fact that we do not speak it in unison, but sing it, only expresses the fact that our spoken words are inadequate to express what we want to say, that the object of our singing reaches far beyond all human words. Nevertheless, we do not mumble unintelligible words; rather we sing words of praise to God, words of thanksgiving, confession, and prayer. Thus the music is completely the servant of the Word. It elucidates the Word in its incomprehensibility.

Because it is completely bound to the Word, the singing of the congregation in its worship service, especially the singing of the house church, is essentially singing in unison. Here words and music combine in a unique way. The freely soaring tone of unison singing finds its sole and essential inner support in the words that are sung. It does not need, therefore, the musical support of other parts. The Bohemian Brethren sang: "With one voice let us sing today, in unison and from the bottom of our heart." "So that together you may with one voice glorify the God and Father of our Lord Jesus Christ" (Rom. 15:6). The essence of all congregational singing on this earth is the purity of unison singing—untouched by the unrelated motives of musical excess—the clarity unclouded by the dark desire to lend musicality an autonomy of its own apart from the words; it is the simplicity and unpretentiousness, the humanness and warmth, of this style of singing. Of course, this truth is only gradually and by patient practice disclosed to our oversophisticated ears. Whether or not a community achieves proper unison singing is a question of its spiritual discernment. This is singing from the heart, singing to the Lord, singing the Word; this is singing in unity.

There are several elements hostile to unison singing, which in the community ought to be very rigorously weeded out. There is no place in the worship service where vanity and bad taste can so assert themselves as in the singing. First, there is the improvised second part that one encounters almost everywhere people are supposed to sing together. It attempts to give the necessary background, the missing richness to the free-floating unison sound and in the process kills both the words and the sound. There are the bass or the alto voices that must call everybody's attention to their astonishing range and therefore sing every hymn an octave lower. There is the solo voice that drowns out everything else, bellowing and quavering at the top of its lungs, reveling in the glory of its own fine organ. There are the less dangerous foes of congregational singing, the "unmusical" who cannot sing, of whom there are far fewer than we are led to believe. Finally, there are often those who will not join in the singing because they are particularly moody or nursing hurt feelings; and thus they disturb the community.

As difficult as it is, unison singing is much less a musical than a spiritual matter. Only where everybody in the community is prepared to assume an attitude of devotion and discipline can unison singing give us the joy that is its alone, even if it exhibits many musical shortcomings.

Primarily the Reformation chorales, as well as the hymns of the Bohemian Brethren and pieces from the historic church, are worth considering for practice in unison singing. Starting here, the community will form an opinion on its own as to which hymns in our hymnbook lend themselves to unison singing and which do not. Any doctrinaire attitude, which we encounter so often in this area, is a bad thing. The decision on this issue can only be made on the merits of each case, and here too we should not become iconoclastic. A community of Christians living together will therefore try hard to master as rich a store of hymns as possible that can be sung without music and from memory. It will achieve this goal if in addition to a freely chosen hymn it inserts in every daily worship service several set verses that can be sung between the readings.

Singing, however, should be practiced not just in the daily worship services, but at regular times during the day or week. The more we sing, the more joy we will derive from it. But, above all, the more concentration and discipline and joy we put into our singing, the richer will be the blessing that will come to the whole life of the community from singing together.

It is the voice of the church that is heard in singing together. It is not I who sing, but the church. However, as a member of the church, I may share in its song. Thus all true singing together must serve to widen our spiritual horizon. It must enable us to recognize our small community as a member of the great Christian church [Christenheit] on earth and must help us willingly and joyfully to take our place in the song of the church with our singing, be it feeble or good.

God's Word, the voice of the church, and our prayer belong together. So we must now speak of prayer together. "If two of you agree about anything you ask for, it will be done for you by my Father in heaven" (Matt. 18:19). There is no part of daily worship together that causes us such serious difficulties and trouble as does common prayer, for here we ourselves are supposed to speak. We have heard God's Word and we have had the privilege of joining in the song of the church, but now we are to pray to God as a community, and this prayer must really be *our* word, *our* prayer—for this day, for our work, for our community, for the particular needs and sins that commonly oppress us, for the persons who are committed to our care. Or should we really not pray for ourselves at all? Should the desire for prayer together with our own lips and in our own words be a forbidden thing? No matter what objections there may be to prayer together, it simply could not be any other way. Christians may and should pray together to God in their own words when they desire to live together under the Word of God. They have requests, gratitude, and intercessions to bring in common to God, and they should do so joyfully and confidently. All our fear of one another, all our inhibitions about praying freely in our own words in the presence of others, can diminish where the common prayer of the community is brought before God by one of its members with dignity and simplicity. Likewise, however, all our observations and criticisms should cease whenever weak words of prayer are offered in the name of Jesus Christ. It is in fact the most normal thing in our common Christian life to pray together. As good and useful as our scruples may be about keeping our prayer pure and biblical, they must nevertheless not stifle the free prayer itself that is so necessary, for it has been endowed with great promise by Jesus Christ.

The extemporaneous prayer at the close of daily worship normally will be said by the head of the house [Hausvater]. But in any case it is best that it always be said by the same person. That places an unexpected responsibility on this person, but in order to safeguard the prayer from the wrong kind of scrutiny and from false subjectivity, one person should pray for all the community for an extended period of time.

The first condition that makes it possible for individuals to pray for the community is the intercession of all the others for such persons and for their praying. How could one person pray the prayer of the community without being held up and supported in prayer by the community itself? At precisely this point every word of criticism must be transformed into more faithful intercession and mutual help. How easily a community can split apart if this is not done!

Extemporaneous prayer in daily worship together should be the prayer of the community and not that of the individual who is praying. It is this individual's task to pray for the community. Thus such a person will have to share the daily life of the community and must know the cares and needs, the joys and thanksgivings, the requests and hopes of the others. The community's work and everything that it involves must not be unknown to the individual who prays for the community. One prays as a believer among other Christians. It will require self-examination and watchfulness if individuals are not to confuse their own hearts with the heart of the community, if a person really is to be guided solely by the task of praying for the community. For this reason it will be good if the persons who have been assigned this task are constantly given the benefit of counsel and help from others in the community, if they receive suggestions and requests to remember this or that need, work, or even a particular person in the prayer. Thus the prayer will become more and more the common prayer of all.

Even extemporaneous prayer will be determined by a certain internal order. It is not the chaotic outburst of a human heart, but the prayer of an internally ordered community. Thus certain prayer requests will recur daily, even if they may perhaps recur in different ways. At first there may be some monotony in the daily repetition of the same petitions that are entrusted to us as a community, but later freedom from an all too individualistic form of prayer will surely be found. If it is possible to add to the number of daily recurring petitions, a weekly order might be tried, as has been proposed on occasion. If that is not possible in the common prayers, it is certainly a help in one's personal times of prayer. Relating the prayer to one of the Scripture readings also will prove helpful for liberating spontaneous prayer from the arbitrariness of subjectivity. This gives support and substance to the prayer.

From time to time a problem will arise where the person given the job of offering prayer for the community feels inwardly unable to offer prayer and would prefer to turn over the task to someone else for the day. However, that is not advisable. Otherwise, the community's prayers will be too easily controlled by moods that have nothing to do with life in the spirit. The persons assigned to pray for the community should learn what it means to have a duty to perform in the congregation even at a time when they would like to avoid this task because they are weighed down by inner emptiness and weariness or by personal guilt. The other members of the community should support them in their weakness, in their inability to pray. Perhaps then the words of Paul will come true: "We do not know how to pray as we ought, but that very Spirit intercedes with sighs too deep for words" (Rom. 8:26). It is of great importance that the community understands, supports, and prays the prayer of these individuals as its own.

The use of set prayers can be a help even for a small community living together under certain circumstances, but often it becomes only an evasion of real prayer. By using ecclesial forms and the church's wealth of thought, we can easily deceive ourselves about our own prayer life. The prayers then become beautiful and profound, but not genuine. As helpful as the church's tradition of prayer is for learning how to pray, nevertheless it cannot take the place of the prayer that I owe to my God today. Here the poorest stammering can be better than the best-phrased prayer. It goes without saying that the state of affairs in public worship services is different from the daily worship of the community living together.

Often in Christian everyday-life communities [Lebensgemeinschaft] there will be a desire for special communities of prayer over and above the prayers in the daily worship together. Here there can probably be no set rule except one—the meetings of such groups should be held only where there is a common desire for them and where it is certain that there will be common participation in a particular prayer service [Gebetstunde]. Any individual undertakings of this kind can easily plant the seed of corruption in the community. It is precisely in this area that it must prove true that the strong support the weak, and the weak not rule over the strong. The New Testament teaches us that a free community of prayer is the most obvious and natural thing and may be viewed without suspicion. But where mistrust and anxiety exist, one must bear with the other in patience. Let nothing be done by force, but everything be done in freedom and love.

We have considered thus far the daily morning worship of Christian everyday-life communities. God's Word, the hymns of the church, and the prayers of the community of faith stand at the beginning of the day. Only when the community has been provided and strengthened with the bread of eternal life does it gather together to receive from God earthly bread for this bodily life. Giving thanks and asking God's blessing, the Christian house church takes its daily bread from the hand of the Lord. Ever since Jesus Christ sat at table with his disciples, the community at the table [Tischgemeinschaft] of Christ's congregation has been blessed by his presence. "When he was at the table with them, he took bread, blessed and broke it, and gave it to them. Then their eyes were opened, and they recognized him" (Luke 24:30–31a). The Scriptures speak of three kinds of community at the table that Jesus keeps with his own: the daily breaking of bread together at meals, the breaking of bread together at the Lord's Supper, and the final breaking of bread together in the reign of God. But in all three, the one thing that counts is that "their eyes were opened and they recognized him." What does it mean to recognize Jesus Christ by way of these gifts? It means, *first*, to recognize Christ as the giver of all gifts, as the Lord and Creator—with the Father and the Holy Spirit—of this our world. Therefore, the community at the table prays "and let *your* gifts to us be blessed,"and thus declares its faith in the eternal deity of Jesus Christ. *Second*, the congregation recognizes that all earthly gifts are given to it only for the sake of Christ, as this whole world is preserved only for the sake of Jesus Christ—for the sake of Christ's Word and its proclamation. Christ is the true bread of life, not only the giver but the gift itself, for whose sake all earthly gifts exist. God patiently preserves us with God's own good gifts only because the Word of Jesus Christ is still to go forth and encounter faith, because our faith is not yet perfected. That is why the Christian congregation breaking bread together at the table prays in Luther's words, "O Lord God, dear heavenly Father, bless us and these your gifts which we receive from your bountiful goodness, through *Jesus Christ our Lord*. Amen"—and thus declares its faith in Jesus Christ as the divine mediator and savior. *Third*, the community of Jesus believes that its Lord desires to be present wherever it asks him to be present. That is why it prays: "Come, Lord Jesus, be our guest," thus confessing the gracious omnipresence of Jesus Christ. Every breaking of bread together fills Christians with gratitude for the present Lord and God, Jesus Christ. It is not as if they were seeking any unhealthy spiritualization of material gifts; rather, in their wholehearted joy in the good gifts of this physical life, Christians recognize their Lord as the true giver of all good gifts. And beyond this, they recognize their Lord as the true gift, the true bread of life itself, and finally as the one who calls them to the joyful banquet in the reign of God. So in a special way, the daily breaking of bread together binds Christians to their Lord and to one another. At the table they recognize their Lord as the one who breaks bread for them. The eyes of their faith are opened.

The breaking of bread together has a festive quality. In the midst of the working day given to us again and again, it is a reminder that God rested after God's work, and that the Sabbath is the meaning and the goal of the week with its toil. Our life is not only a great deal of trouble and hard work; it is also refreshment and joy in God's goodness. We labor, but God nourishes and sustains us. That is a reason to celebrate. People should not eat the bread of anxious toil (Ps. 127:2). Rather "eat your bread with enjoyment" (Eccles. 9:7), "so I commend enjoyment, for there is nothing better for people under the sun than to eat, and drink, and enjoy themselves" (Eccles. 8:15). But of course, "apart from him, who can eat or who can have enjoyment?" (Eccles. 2:25). It is said of the seventy elders of Israel who climbed Mount Sinai with Moses and Aaron that "they beheld God, and they ate and drank" (Exod. 24:11). God will not tolerate the unfestive, joyless manner in which we eat our bread with sighs of groaning, with pompous, self-important busyness, or even with shame. Through the daily meal God is calling us to rejoice, to celebrate in the midst of our working day.

Christian community at the table also signifies obligation. It is *our* daily bread that we eat, not my own. We share our bread. Thus we are firmly bound to one another not only in the Spirit, but with our whole physical being. The *one* bread that is given to our community unites us in a firm covenant. Now no one must hunger as long as the other has bread, and whoever shatters this community of our bodily life also shatters the community of the Spirit. Both are inextricably linked together. "Share your bread with the hungry" (Isa. 58:7). "Do not despise the hungry" (Sirach 4:2), for the Lord meets us in the hungry (Matt. 25:37). "If a brother or sister is naked and lacks daily food, and one of you says to them, 'Go in peace; keep warm and eat your fill,' and yet you do not supply their bodily needs, what is the good of that?" (James 2:15f.). As long as we eat our bread together, we will have enough even with the smallest amount. Hunger begins only when people desire to keep their own bread for themselves. That is a strange divine law. Could not the story of the miraculous feeding of the 5,000 with two fish and five loaves of bread also have this meaning, along with many others?

The breaking of bread together teaches Christians that here they still eat the perishable bread of the earthly pilgrimage. But if they share this bread with one another, they will also one day receive together imperishable bread in the Father's house. "Blessed is the one who will eat bread in the reign of God" (Luke 14:15).

After the first morning hour, the Christian's day until evening belongs to *work*. "People go out to their work and to their labor until the evening" (Ps. 104:23). In most cases a community of Christians living together will separate for the duration of the working hours. Praying and working are two different things. Prayer should not be hindered by work, but neither should work be hindered by prayer. Just as it was God's will that human beings should work six days and rest and celebrate before the face of God on the seventh, so it is also God's will that every day should be marked for the Christian both by prayer and work. Prayer also requires its own time. But the longest part of the day belongs to work. The inseparable unity of both will only become clear when work and prayer each receives its own undivided due. Without the burden and labor of the day, prayer is not prayer; and without prayer, work is not work. Only the Christian knows that. Thus it is precisely in the clear distinction between them that their oneness becomes apparent.

Work puts human beings in the world of things. It requires achievement from them. Christians step out of the world of personal encounter into the world of impersonal things, the "It"; and this new encounter frees them for objectivity, for the world of the It is only an instrument in the hand of God for the purification of Christians from all self-absorption and selfishness. The work of the world can only be accomplished where people forget themselves, where they lose themselves in a cause, reality, the task, the It. Christians learn at work to allow the task to set the bounds for them. Thus, for them, work becomes a remedy for the lethargy and laziness of the flesh.

The demands of the flesh die in the world of things. But that can only happen where Christians break through the It to the "You" ["Du"] of God, who commands the work and the deed and makes them serve to liberate Christians from themselves. In this process work does not cease to be work; but the severity and rigor of labor is sought all the more by those who know what good it does them. The continuing conflict with the It remains. But at the same time the breakthrough has been made. The unity of prayer and work, the unity of the day, is found because finding the You of God behind the It of the day's work is what Paul means by his admonition to "pray without ceasing" (1 Thess. 5:17). The prayer of the Christian reaches, therefore, beyond the time allocated to it and extends into the midst of the work. It surrounds the whole day, and in so doing, it does not hinder the work; it promotes work, affirms work, gives work great significance and joyfulness. Thus every word, every deed, every piece of work of the Christian becomes a prayer, not in the unreal sense of being constantly distracted from the task that must be done, but in a real breakthrough from the hard It to the gracious You [Du]. "And whatever you do, in word or deed, do everything in the name of the Lord Jesus" (Col. 3:17).

The whole day now acquires an order and a discipline gained by winning this unity of the day. This order and discipline must be sought and found in the morning prayer. It will stand the test at work. Prayer offered in early morning is decisive for the day. The wasted time we are ashamed of, the temptations we succumb to, the weakness and discouragement in our work, the disorder and lack of discipline in our thinking and in our dealings with other people—all these very frequently have their cause in our neglect of morning prayer. The ordering and scheduling of our time will become more secure when it comes from prayer. The temptations of the working day will be overcome by this breakthrough to God. The decisions that are demanded by our work will become simpler and easier when they are made not in fear of other people, but solely before the face of God. "Whatever you do, do it from your hearts, as done for the Lord and not done for human beings" (Col. 3:23). Even routine mechanical work will be performed more patiently when it comes from the knowledge of God and God's command. Our strength and energy for work increase when we have asked God to give us the strength we need for our daily work.

Where it is possible, the midday hour becomes for a community of Christians living together a brief rest on their journey through the day. Half of the day is past. The congregation thanks God and asks for protection until evening. It receives its daily bread and prays in the words of a Reformation hymn: "Feed your children, God most holy, / Comfort sinners poor and lowly." It is God who must feed us. We cannot and dare not take it for ourselves because we poor sinners have not merited it. Thus the meal God serves us becomes a consolation for the afflicted, for it is proof of the grace and faithfulness with which God preserves and guides God's children. It is true that the Scripture says that "anyone unwilling to work should not eat" (2 Thess. 3:10) and thus makes the receiving of bread strictly dependent on working for it. But the Scriptures do not say anything about any claim that working persons have on God for their bread. It is true that work is commanded, but the bread is God's free and gracious gift. We cannot simply take it for granted that our own work provides us with bread; rather this is God's order of grace. The day belongs to God alone. Hence in the middle of the day, the Christian community of faith gathers and lets God invite them to the table. The midday hour is one of the seven prayer hours of the church and of the singer of the Psalms. At the height of the day the church invokes the triune God in praise of God's wonders and in prayer for help and speedy redemption. At midday the heavens were darkened above the cross of Jesus. The work of atonement was approaching its completion. Where a community of Christians living together is able to be together at this hour for a brief daily worship time of song and prayer, it will not do so in vain.

The day's work comes to an end. When the day has been hard and toilsome, the Christian will understand what Paul Gerhardt meant when he sang: "Head, hands and feet so tired, / Are glad the day's expired, / That work comes to an end; / My heart is fill'd with gladness / That God from all earth's sadness, / And from sin's toil relief will send." One day is long enough to keep one's faith; the next day will have its own worries.

The community of Christians living together gathers together again. The evening breaking of bread together and the final daily worship service bring them together. With the disciples in Emmaus they ask: "Lord, stay with us, because it is almost evening and the day is now nearly over." It is a good thing if the daily evening worship can really be held at the end of the day, thus becoming the last word before the night's rest. When night falls, the true light of God's Word shines brighter for the community of faith. The prayer of the Psalms, a Scripture reading, a hymn, and a prayer together close the day as they opened it. We still need to say a few words on the subject of evening prayer. This is the special place for intercession together. After the day's work has been completed, we ask for God's blessing, peace, and preservation for the whole of Christianity, for our congregation, for pastors in their ministries, for the poor, the wretched and lonely, for the sick and dying, for our neighbors, for our family at home, and for our community. When could we ever have a deeper awareness of God's power and working than in the hour when we lay aside our own work and entrust ourselves to God's faithful hands? When are we more prepared to pray for blessing, peace, and preservation than the time when our activity is at an end? When we grow tired, God works. "The Guardian of Israel neither slumbers nor sleeps." Our request for the forgiveness of every wrong we have done to God and to one another, for god's forgiveness and that of our brothers, and for the willingness gladly to forgive any wrong done to us, belongs then, too, especially in the evening prayers of a community of Christians living together. It is an old custom of the monasteries that by set practice in the daily evening worship the abbot asks his brothers to forgive him for all the sins of omission and wrongdoings committed against them. After the brothers assure him of their forgiveness, they likewise ask the abbot to forgive them for their sins of omission and wrongdoings and receive his forgiveness. "Do not let the sun go down on your anger" (Eph. 4:26). It is a decisive rule of every Christian community that every division that the day has caused must be healed in the evening. It is perilous for the Christian to go to bed with an unreconciled heart. Therefore, it is a good idea especially to include the request for mutual forgiveness in every evening's prayers, so that reconciliation can be achieved and renewal of the community established. Finally, in all the old evening prayers, it is striking how frequently we encounter their plea for preservation during the night from the devil, from terror and from an evil, sudden death. The ancients were keenly aware of human helplessness while sleeping, the kinship of sleep with death, and the devil's cunning in causing our downfall when we are defenseless. That is why they prayed for the assistance of the holy angels and their golden weapons, for the presence of the heavenly hosts at the time when Satan would gain power over us. Most remarkable and profound is the ancient church's request that, when our eyes are closed in sleep, God may nevertheless keep our hearts alert to god. It is a prayer that God may dwell with us and in us, even when we feel and know nothing, that God may keep our hearts pure and holy in spite of all the worries and temptations of the night, that God may prepare our hearts to hear the call at any time and, like the boy Samuel, answer even in the night, "Speak, Lord, for your servant is listening" (1 Sam. 3:10). Even while sleeping we are in the hands of God or in the power of the evil one. Even while we sleep, God can perform miracles upon us or the evil one can cause devastation in us. So we pray in the evening: "Though our eyes in sleep will close, / May our hearts in you repose, / Protect us, God, with your right arm, / And shield our souls from sin's cruel harm" (Luther). But the word of the Psalter stands over the morning and the evening: "Yours is the day, yours also the night" (Ps. 74:16).

Morning Prayer

Scriptures

Psalms
as a Community

Singing

Must Know Scriptures to help others?

Breaking of the Bread

36

5\ Help DM Prayer

The Day Alone

"The praise of silence befits you, O God, in Zion" (Ps. 65:2 [1]).
Many persons seek community because they are afraid of loneliness
[der Einsamkeit]. Because they can no longer endure being alone,
such people are driven to seek the company of others. Christians,
too, who cannot cope on their own, and who in their own lives
have had some bad experiences, hope to experience help with this
in the company of other people. More often than not, they are
disappointed. They then blame the community for what is really their
own fault. The Christian community is not a spiritual sanatorium.
Those who take refuge in community while fleeing from themselves
are misusing it to indulge in empty talk and distraction, no matter
how spiritual this idle talk and distraction may appear. In reality
they are not seeking community at all, but only a thrill that will
allow them to forget their isolation [Vereinsamung] for a short time.
It is precisely such misuse of community that creates the deadly
isolation of human beings. Such attempts to find healing result in
the undermining of speech and all genuine experience and, finally,
resignation and spiritual death.

Whoever cannot be alone [allein] should beware of community. Such
people will only do harm to themselves and to the community. Alone
you stood before God when God called you. Alone you had to obey

God's voice. Alone you had to take up your cross, struggle, and pray and alone you will die and give an account to God. You cannot avoid yourself, for it is precisely God who has singled you out. If you do not want to be alone, you are rejecting Christ's call to you, and you can have no part in the community of those who are called. "The confrontation with death and its demands comes to us all; no one can die for another. All must fight their own battle with death by themselves, alone. I will not be with you then, nor you with me" (Luther).

But the reverse is also true. *Whoever cannot stand being in community should beware of being alone.* You are called into the community of faith; the call was not meant for you alone. You carry your cross, you struggle, and you pray in the community of faith, the community of those who are called. You are not alone even when you die, and on the day of judgment you will be only one member of the great community of faith of Jesus Christ. If you neglect the community of other Christians, you reject the call of Jesus Christ, and thus your being alone [Alleinsein] can only become harmful for you. "If I die, then I am not alone in death; if I suffer, they (the community of faith) suffer with me" (Luther).

We recognize, then, that only as we stand within the community can we be alone, and only those who are alone can live in the community. Both belong together. Only in the community do we learn to be properly alone [allein]; and only in being alone [Alleinsein] do we learn to live properly in the community. It is not as if the one preceded the other; rather both begin at the same time, namely, with the call of Jesus Christ.

Each taken by itself has profound pitfalls and perils. Those who want community without solitude [Alleinsein] plunge into the void of words and feelings, and those who seek solitude without community perish in the bottomless pit of vanity, self-infatuation, and despair.

Whoever cannot be alone should beware of community. Whoever cannot stand being in community should beware of being alone.

The day together of Christians who live in community is accompanied by each individual's day alone. That is the way it must be. The day together will be unfruitful without the day alone, both for the community and for the individual.

The mark of solitude [Einsamkeit] is silence, just as speech is the mark of community. Silence and speech have the same inner connection and distinction as do being alone [Alleinsein] and community. One does not exist without the other. Genuine speech comes out of silence, and genuine silence comes out of speech.

Silence does not mean being incapable of speech, just as speech does not mean idle talk. Being incapable of speech does not create solitude, and idle talk does not create community. "Silence is the excess, the inebriation, the sacrifice of speech. But being incapable of speech is not holy; it is like a thing that has only been mutilated, not sacrificed. Zachary was incapable of speech, rather than being silent. If he had accepted the revelation, he may perhaps have come out of the temple not incapable of speaking, but silent" (Ernest Hello). That speaking which reestablishes and binds the community together is accompanied by silence. "There is a time . . . to keep silence and a time to speak" (Eccles. 3:7). Just as there are certain times in a Christian's day for speaking the Word, particularly the time of daily worship and prayer together, so the day also needs certain times of silence under the Word and silence that comes out of the Word. These will mainly be the times before and after hearing the Word. The Word comes not to the noisemakers but to those who are silent. The stillness of the temple is the sign of God's holy presence in the Word.

There is an indifferent or even negative attitude toward silence which sees in it a disparagement of God's revelation in the Word. Silence is misunderstood as a solemn gesture, as a mystical desire to get beyond the Word. Silence is no longer seen in its essential relationship to the Word, as the simple act of the individual who falls silent under the Word of God. We are silent before hearing the Word because our thoughts are already focused on the Word, as children are quiet when they enter their father's room. We are silent after hearing the Word because the Word is still speaking and living and dwelling within us. We are silent early in the morning because God should have the first word, and we are silent before going to bed because the last word also belongs to God. We remain silent solely for the sake of the Word, not thereby to dishonor the Word but rather to honor and receive it properly. In the end, silence means nothing other than waiting for God's Word and coming from God's Word with a blessing. But everybody knows this is something that needs to be learned in these days when idle talk has gained the upper hand. Real silence, real stillness, really holding one's tongue, comes only as the sober consequence of spiritual silence.

This silence before the Word, however, will have an impact on the whole day. If we have learned to be silent before the Word, we will also learn to manage our silence and our speech during the day. Silence can be forbidden, self-satisfied, haughty, or insulting. From this it follows that silence in itself can never be the issue. The silence of the Christian is listening silence, humble stillness that may be broken at any time for the sake of humility. It is silence in conjunction with the Word. This is what Thomas à Kempis meant when he said: "No one speaks more confidently than the one who gladly remains silent." There is a wonderful power in being silent—the power of clarification, purification, and focus on what is essential. This is true even when considered from a purely profane point of view. But silence before the Word leads to proper hearing and thus also to proper speaking of God's Word at the right time. Much that is unnecessary remains unsaid. But what is essential and helpful can be said in a few words.

When a community lives close together in a confined space and outwardly cannot give the individual the necessary quiet, then regular times of silence are absolutely essential. After a period of silence, we encounter others in a different and fresh way. Many a community living together will only be able to ensure the individual's right to be alone by adopting a set daily discipline, and thereby will keep the community itself from harm.

We will not discuss here all the wonderful fruits that can come to Christians in solitude [Alleinsein] and silence. It is all too easy to go dangerously astray in this matter. We could also probably cite many a dubious experience that can grow out of silence. Silence can be a dreadful wasteland with all its isolated stretches and terrors. It can also be a paradise of self-deception. One is not better than the other. Be that as it may, let none expect from silence anything but a simple encounter with the Word of God for the sake of which Christians have entered into silence. This encounter, however, is given to them as a gift. Their silence will be richly rewarded if they do not set any conditions on how they expect this encounter to take place or what they hope to get from it, but simply accept it as it comes.

There are three things for which the Christian needs a regular time alone during the day: *meditation on the Scripture, prayer*, and *intercession*. All three should find a place in the *daily period of meditation*. There is no reason to be concerned about the use of this word "meditation." In this case we are making our own an old word of the church and the Reformation.

One might ask why a special time is needed for this, since we already have everything we need in daily worship together. In the following we will arrive at the answer to this question.

The period of meditation is useful for personal consideration of Scripture, personal prayer, and personal intercession. It serves no other purpose. Spiritual experiments have no place here. But there must be time for these three things, because it is precisely God who requires them of us. Even if for a long time meditation were to mean nothing but that we are performing a service we owe to God, this would be reason enough to do it.

This time for meditation does not allow us to sink into the void and bottomless pit of aloneness [Alleinsein], rather it allows us to be alone [allein] with the Word. In so doing it gives us solid ground on which to stand and clear guidance for the steps we have to take.

Whereas in our daily worship together we read long, continuous texts, in our personal meditation on Scripture we stick to a brief selected text that will possibly remain unchanged for an entire week. If in our communal reading of the Scriptures we are led more into the whole length and breadth of the Holy Scriptures, here we are guided into the unfathomable depths of a particular sentence and word. Both are equally necessary, "that you may have the power to comprehend, with all the saints, what is the breadth and length and height and depth" (Eph. 3:18).

In our meditation we read the text given to us on the strength of the promise that it has something quite personal to say to us for this day and for our standing as Christians—it is not only God's Word for the community of faith, but also God's Word for me personally. We expose ourselves to the particular sentence and word until we personally are affected by it. When we do that, we are doing nothing but what the simplest, most unlearned Christian does every day. We are reading the Word of God as God's Word for us. Therefore, we do not ask what this text has to say to other people. For those of us who are preachers that means we will not ask how we would preach or teach on this text, but what it has to say to us personally. It is true that to do this we must first have understood the content of the text. But in this situation we are neither doing an exegesis of the text, nor preparing a sermon or conducting a Bible study of any kind; we are rather waiting for God's Word to us. We are not waiting in vain; on the contrary, we are waiting on the basis of a clear promise. Often we are so burdened and overwhelmed with other thoughts, images, and concerns that it may take a long time before God's Word has cleared all that away and gets through to us. But it will surely come, just as surely as none other than God has come to human beings and wants to come again. For that very reason we will begin our meditation with the prayer that God may send the Holy Spirit to us through the Word, and reveal God's Word to us, and enlighten our minds.

It is not necessary for us to get through the entire text in one period of meditation. Often we will have to stick to a single sentence or even to one word because we have been gripped and challenged by it and can no longer evade it. Are not the words "father," "love," "mercy," "cross," "sanctification," or "resurrection" often enough to fill amply the brief time set aside for our meditation?

It is not necessary for us to be anxious about putting our thoughts and prayers into words as we meditate. Silent thinking and praying, which comes only from our listening, can often be more beneficial.

It is not necessary for us to find new ideas in our meditation. Often that only distracts us and satisfies our vanity. It is perfectly sufficient if the Word enters in and dwells within us as we read and understand it. As Mary "pondered . . . in her heart" what the shepherds told her, as a person's words often stick in our mind for a long time—as they dwell and work within us, preoccupy us, disturb us, or make us happy without our being able to do anything about it—so as we meditate,

God's Word desires to enter in and stay with us. It desires to move us, to work in us, and to make such an impression on us that the whole day long we will not get away from it. Then it will do its work in us, often without our being aware of it.

Above all, it is not necessary for us to have any unexpected, extraordinary experiences while meditating. That can happen, but if it does not, this is not a sign that the period of meditation has been unprofitable. Not only at the beginning, but time and again a great inner dryness and lack of concern will make itself felt in us, a listlessness, even an inability to meditate. We must not get stuck in such experiences. Above all, we must not allow them to dissuade us from observing our period of meditation with great patience and fidelity. That is why it is not good for us to take too seriously the many bad experiences we have with ourselves during the time of meditation. It is here that our old vanity and the wrongful demands we make on God could sneak into our lives in a pious, roundabout way, as if it were our right to have nothing but edifying and blissful experiences, and as if the discovery of our inner poverty were beneath our dignity. But we will not make any headway with such an attitude. Impatience and self-reproach only foster our complacency and entangle us ever more deeply in the net of introspection. But there is no more time to observe ourselves in meditation than there is in the Christian life as a whole. We should pay attention to the Word alone and leave it to the Word to deal effectively with everything. For may it not be the case that it is none other than God who sends us these hours of emptiness and dryness, so that we might once again expect everything from God's Word? "Seek God, not happiness"—that is the fundamental rule of all meditation. If you seek God alone, you will gain happiness—that is the promise of all meditation.

The consideration of Scripture leads into prayer. We have already said that the most promising way to pray is to allow oneself to be guided by the words of the Bible, to pray on the basis of the words of Scripture. In this way we will not fall prey to our own emptiness. Prayer means nothing else but the readiness to appropriate the Word, and what is more, to let it speak to me in my personal situation, in my particular tasks, decisions, sins, and temptations. What can never enter the prayer of the community may here silently be made known to God. On the basis of the words of Scripture we pray that God may throw light on our day, preserve us from sin, and enable us to grow in holiness, and that we may be faithful in our work and have the strength to do it. And we may be certain that our prayer will be heard because it issues from God's Word and promise. Because God's Word has found its fulfillment in Jesus Christ, all the prayers we pray on the basis of this Word are certainly fulfilled and answered in Jesus Christ.

A special difficulty in the time of meditation is that it is so easy for our thoughts to wander and go their own way, toward other persons or to some events in our life. As much as this may sadden and shame us, we must not become despondent and anxious, or even conclude that meditation is really not something for us. If we find ourselves in this situation, it is often a help not frantically to restrain our thoughts, but quite calmly to draw into our prayer those people and events toward which our thoughts keep turning, and thus patiently to return to the starting point of the meditation.

Just as we tie our personal prayers to the words of the Bible, we do the same with our intercessions. It is not possible to remember in the intercessory prayers of daily worship together all the persons who are entrusted to our care, or at any rate to do it in the way that is required of us. All Christians have their own circle of those who have requested them to intercede on their behalf, or people for whom for various reasons they know they have been called upon to pray. First of all, this circle will include those with whom they must live every day. With this we have advanced to the point at which we hear the heartbeat of all Christian life together. A Christian community either lives by the intercessory prayers of its members for one another, or the community will be destroyed. I can no longer condemn or hate other Christians for whom I pray, no matter how much trouble they cause me. In intercessory prayer the face that may have been strange and intolerable to me is transformed into the face of one for whom Christ died, the face of a pardoned sinner. That is a blessed discovery for the Christian who is beginning to offer intercessory prayer for others. As far as we are concerned, there is no dislike, no personal tension, no disunity or strife, that cannot be overcome by intercessory prayer. Intercessory prayer is the purifying bath into which the individual and the community must enter every day. We may struggle hard with one another in intercessory prayer, but that struggle has the promise of achieving its goal.

How does that happen? Offering intercessory prayer means nothing other than Christians bringing one another into the presence of God, seeing each other under the cross of Jesus as poor human beings and sinners in need of grace. Then, everything about other people that repels me falls away. Then I see them in all their need, hardship, and distress. Their need and their sin become so heavy and oppressive to me that I feel as if they were my own, and I can do nothing else but bid: Lord, you yourself, you alone, deal with them according to your firmness and your goodness. Offering intercessory prayer means granting other Christians the same right we have received, namely, the right to stand before Christ and to share in Christ's mercy.

Thus it is clear that intercessory prayer is also a daily service Christians owe to God and one another. Those who deny their neighbors prayers of intercession deny them a service Christians are called to perform. Furthermore, it is clear that intercessory prayer is not something general and vague, but something very concrete. It is interested in specific persons and specific difficulties and therefore specific requests. The more concrete my intercessory prayer becomes, the more promising it is.

Finally, we can no longer close our eyes to the realization that the ministry of intercession demands time of every Christian, but most of all of the pastor on whom the needs of the whole community of faith rest. Intercessory prayer alone would occupy the entire time of daily meditation if it were done properly. All this proves that intercessory prayer is a gift of God's grace for every Christian community and for every Christian. Because God has made us such an immeasurably great offer here, we should accept it joyfully. The very time we give to intercession will turn out to be a daily source of new joy in God and in the Christian congregation.

Because consideration of the Scriptures, prayer, and intercession involve a service that is our duty, and because the grace of God can be found in this service, we should train ourselves to set a regular time during the day for them, just as we do for every other service we perform. That is not "legalism," but discipline and faithfulness. For most people, the early morning will prove to be the best time. We have a right to this time, even prior to the claims of other people, and we may demand it as a completely undisturbed quiet time despite all external pressures. For the pastor, it is an indispensable duty on which the whole practice of ministry will depend. Who can really be faithful in great things, if they have not learned to be faithful in the things of daily life?

Every day brings the Christian many hours of being alone in an unchristian environment. These are times of *testing*. This is the proving ground of a genuine time of meditation and genuine Christian community. Has the community served to make individuals free, strong, and mature, or has it made them insecure and dependent? Has it taken them by the hand for a while so that they would learn again to walk by themselves, or has it made them anxious and unsure? This is one of the toughest and most serious questions that can be put to any form of everyday Christian life in community [Lebensgemeinschaft]. Moreover, we will see at this point whether Christians' time of meditation has led them into an unreal world from which they awaken with a fright when they step out into the workaday world, or whether it has led them into the real world of God from which they enter into the day's activities strengthened and purified. Has it transported them for a few short moments into a spiritual ecstasy that vanishes when everyday life returns, or has it planted the Word of God so soberly and so deeply in their heart that it holds and strengthens them all day long, leading them to active love, to obedience, to good works? Only the day can decide. Is the invisible presence of the Christian community a reality and a help to the individual? Do the intercessory prayers of the others carry me through the day? Is the Word of God close to me as a comfort and a strength? Or do I misuse my solitude [Alleinsein] against the community, against the Word and prayer? Individuals must be aware that even their hours of being alone [Alleinsein] reverberate through the community. In their solitude they can shatter and tarnish the community or they can strengthen and sanctify it. Every act of self-discipline by a Christian is also a service to the community. Conversely, there is no sin in thought, word, or deed, no matter how personal or secret, that does not harm the whole community. When the cause of an illness gets into one's body, whether or not anyone knows where it comes from, or in what member it has lodged, the body is made ill. This is the appropriate metaphor for the Christian community. Every member serves the whole body, contributing either to its health or to its ruin, for we *are* members of one body not only when we want to be, but in our whole existence. This is not a theory, but a spiritual reality that is often experienced in the Christian community with shocking clarity, sometimes destructively and sometimes beneficially.

Those who return to the community of Christians who live together, after a successful day, bring with them the blessing of their solitude, but they themselves receive anew the blessing of the community. Blessed are those who are alone in the strength of the community. Blessed are those who preserve community in the strength of solitude. But the strength of solitude and the strength of community is the strength of the Word of God alone, which is meant for the individual in the community.

A page to explain on

Silent PRAYER!

Intercessory Prayer

Service

"An argument started among the disciples as to which of them would be the greatest" (Luke 9:46). We know who sows this dissension in the Christian community. But perhaps we do not think enough about the fact that no Christian community ever comes together without this argument appearing as a seed of discord. No sooner are people together than they begin to observe, judge, and classify each other. Thus, even as Christian community is in the process of being formed, an invisible, often unknown, yet terrible life-and-death struggle commences. "An argument started among them"—this is enough to destroy a community. It is vitally necessary, therefore, that every Christian community keep an eye on this dangerous enemy from the very outset and eradicate it. There is no time to lose here, because from the first moment two people meet, one begins looking for a competitive position to assume and hold against the other. There are strong people and weak ones. If people are not strong, they immediately claim the right of the weak as their own and use it against the strong. People are talented and untalented, simple and difficult, devout and less devout, sociable and loners. Does not the untalented person have a position to assume just as well as the talented person, the difficult person just as well as the simple one? And if I am not talented, then perhaps I am, nonetheless, devout, or if I am not devout, it is only because I do not want to be. May not the sociable individuals win everyone over to their side and compromise the loner? And yet, may not the loner become the invincible enemy and ultimate conqueror of the sociable individual? Are there any people who do not with instinctive assurance find the place where they can stand and defend themselves, but which they will never give up to another, for which they will fight with all the natural drive to self-assertion? All this can occur in the most respectable or even the most pious forms. But it is really important for a Christian community to know that somewhere in it there will certainly be an "argument among the disciples as to which of them would be the greatest." It is the struggle of natural human beings for self-justification. They find it only by comparing themselves with others, by condemning and judging others. Self-justification and judging belong together in the same way that justification by grace and serving belong together.

Often we combat our evil thoughts most effectively if we absolutely refuse to allow them to be verbalized. It is certain that the spirit of self-justification can only be overcome by the spirit of grace; and it is just as certain that the individual judgmental thought can be limited and suppressed by never allowing it to be spoken except as a confession of sin, which we will talk about later. Those who keep their tongue in check control both spirit and body (James 3:3ff.). Thus it must be a decisive rule of all Christian community life that each individual is prohibited from talking about another Christian in secret. It is clear and will be shown in what follows that this prohibition does not include the word of admonition that is spoken personally to another. However, talking about others in secret is not allowed even under the pretense of help and goodwill. For it is precisely in this guise that the spirit of hatred between believers always creeps in, seeking to cause trouble. This is not the place to specify the limitations placed on such a rule in particular cases.

They are subject to decisions made in each instance. However, the point is clear and biblical. "You sit and speak against your kin; you slander your own mother's child. . . .But now I rebuke you, and lay the charge before you" (Ps. 50:20f.). "Do not speak evil against one another, brothers and sisters. Whoever speaks evil against another or judges another, speaks evil against the law and judges the law; but if you judge the law, you are not a doer of the law but a judge. There is one lawgiver and judge who is able to save and to destroy. So who, then, are you to judge your neighbor?" (James 4:11–12). "Let no evil talk come out of your mouths, but only what is useful for building up, as there is need, so that your words may give grace to those who hear" (Eph. 4:29).

Where this discipline of the tongue is practiced right from the start, individuals will make an amazing discovery. They will be able to stop constantly keeping an eye on others, judging them, condemning them, and putting them in their places and thus doing violence to them. They can now allow other Christians to live freely, just as God has brought them face to face with each other. The view of such persons expands and, to their amazement, they recognize for the first time the richness of God's creative glory shining over their brothers and sisters. God did not make others as I would have made them. God did not give them to me so that I could dominate and control them, but so that I might find the Creator by means of them. Now other people, in the freedom with which they were created, become an occasion for me to rejoice, whereas before they were only a nuisance and trouble for me. God does not want me to mold others into the image that seems good to me, that is, into my own image. Instead, in their freedom from me God made other people in God's own image. I can never know in advance how God's image should appear in others. That image always takes on a completely new and unique form whose origin is found solely in God's free and sovereign act of creation. To me that form may seem strange, even ungodly. But God creates every person in the image of God's Son, the Crucified, and this image, likewise, certainly looked strange and ungodly to me before I grasped it.

Strong and weak, wise or foolish, talented or untalented, pious or less pious, the complete diversity of individuals in the community is no longer a reason to talk and judge and condemn, and therefore no longer a pretext for self-justification. Rather this diversity is a reason for rejoicing in one another and serving one another. Even in this new situation all the members of the community are given their special place; this is no longer the place, however, in which they can most successfully promote themselves, but the place where they can best carry out their service. In a Christian community, everything depends on whether each individual is an indispensable link in a chain. The chain is unbreakable only when even the smallest link holds tightly with the others. A community that allows the presence of members who do nothing be destroyed by them. Thus it is a good idea that all members receive a definite task to perform for the community, so that they may know in times of doubt that they too are not useless and incapable of doing anything. Every Christian community must know that not only do the weak need the strong, but also that the strong cannot exist without the weak. The elimination of the weak is the death of the community.

The Christian community should not be governed by self-justification, which violates others, but by justification by grace, which serves others. Once individuals have experienced the mercy of God in their lives, from then on they desire only to serve. The proud throne of the judge no longer lures them; instead they want to be down among the wretched and lowly, because God found them down there themselves. "Do not be haughty, but associate with the lowly" (Rom. 12:16).

Those who would learn to serve must first learn to think little of themselves. "[You should] not . . . think of yourself more highly than you ought to think" (Rom. 12:3). "The highest and most useful lesson is to truly know yourself and to think humbly of yourself. Making nothing of yourself and always having a good opinion of others is great wisdom and perfection" (Thomas à Kempis). "Do not claim to be wiser than you are" (Rom. 12:17). Only those who live by the forgiveness of their sin in Jesus Christ will think little of themselves in the right way. They will know that their own wisdom completely came to an end when Christ forgave them. They remember the cleverness of the first human beings, who wanted to know what is good and evil and died in this cleverness. The first person, however, who was born on this earth was Cain, the murderer of his brother. His crime is the fruit of humanity's wisdom. Because they can no longer consider themselves wise, Christians will also have a modest opinion of their own plans and intentions. They will know that it is good for their own will to be broken in their encounter with their neighbor. They will be ready to consider their neighbor's will more important and urgent than their own. What does it matter if our own plans are thwarted? Is it not better to serve our neighbor than to get our own way?

Not only the will, but also the honor of the other is more important than my own. "How can you believe when you accept glory from one another and do not seek the glory that comes from the one who alone is God?" (John 5:44). The desire for one's own honor hinders faith. Those who seek their own honor are no longer seeking God and their neighbor. What does it matter if I suffer injustice? Would I not have deserved even more severe punishment from God if God had not treated me with mercy? Is not justice done to me a thousand times over even in injustice? Must it not be beneficial and conducive to humility for me to learn to bear such petty ills silently and patiently? "Patience is better than pride" (Eccles. 7:8). Those who live by justification by grace are prepared to accept even insults and slights without protest, taking them as from God's chastising and gracious hand. It is not a good sign when we can no longer stand to hear such things without immediately recalling that even Paul insisted on his rights as a Roman citizen and that Jesus replied to the man who struck him, "Why do you strike me?" In any case, none of us will really act as Jesus and Paul did if we have not first learned like them to keep silent amidst insults and humiliations. The sin of irritability that blossoms so quickly in the community shows again and again how much inordinate ambition, and thus how much unbelief, still exists in the community.

Finally, one extreme statement must still be made, without any platitudes, and in all soberness. Not considering oneself wise, but associating with the lowly, means considering oneself the worst of sinners. This arouses total opposition not only from those who live at the level of nature, but also from Christians who are self-aware. It sounds like an exaggeration, an untruth. Yet even Paul said of himself that he was the foremost, i.e., the worst of sinners (1 Tim. 1:15). He said this at the very place in scripture where he was speaking of his ministry as an apostle. There can be no genuine knowledge of sin that does not lead me down to this depth. If my sin appears to me to be in any way smaller or less reprehensible in comparison with the sins of others, then I am not yet recognizing my sin at all. My sin is of necessity the worst, the most serious, the most objectionable. Christian love will find any number of excuses for the sins of others; only for my sin is there no excuse whatsoever. That is why my sin is the worst. Those who would serve others in the community must descend all the way down to this depth of humility. How could I possibly serve other persons in unfeigned humility if their sins appear to me to be seriously worse than my own? If I am to have any hope for them, then I must not raise myself above them. Such service would be a sham. "Do not believe that you have made any progress in the work of sanctification, if you do not feel deeply that you are less than all others" (Thomas à Kempis).

How, then, is true Christian service performed in the Christian community? We are inclined these days to reply too quickly that the one real service to our neighbor is to serve them with the Word of God. It is true that there is no service that can equal this one, and even more, that every other service is oriented to the service of the Word. Yet a Christian community does not consist solely of preachers of the Word. The improper use of this could become oppressive if several other things were overlooked at this point.

The *first* service one owes to others in the community involves listening to them. Just as our love for God begins with listening to God's Word, the beginning of love for other Christians is learning to listen to them. God's love for us is shown by the fact that God not only gives us God's Word, but also lends us God's ear. We do God's work for our brothers and sisters when we learn to listen to them. So often Christians, especially preachers, think that their only service is always to have to "offer" something when they are together with other people. They forget that listening can be a greater service than speaking. Many people seek a sympathetic ear and do not find it among Christians, because these Christians are talking even when they should be listening. But Christians who can no longer listen to one another will soon no longer be listening to God either; they will always be talking even in the presence of God. The death of the spiritual life starts here, and in the end there is nothing left but empty spiritual chatter and clerical condescension which chokes on pious words. Those who cannot listen long and patiently will always be talking past others, and finally no longer will even notice it. Those who think their time is too precious to spend listening will never really have time for God and others, but only for themselves and for their own words and plans.

For Christians, pastoral care differs essentially from preaching in that here the task of listening is joined to the task of speaking the Word. There is also a kind of listening with half an ear that presumes already to know what the other person has to say. This impatient, inattentive listening really despises the other Christian and finally is only waiting to get a chance to speak and thus to get rid of the other. This sort of listening is no fulfillment of our task. And it is certain that here, too, in our attitude toward other Christians we simply see reflected our own relationship to God. It should be no surprise that we are no longer able to perform the greatest service of listening that God has entrusted to us—hearing the confession of another Christian—if we refuse to lend our ear to another person on lesser subjects. The pagan world [heidnische Welt] today knows something about persons who often can be helped only by having someone who will seriously listen to them. On this insight it has built its own secular form of pastoral care [säkularisierte Seelsorge], which has become popular with many people, including Christians. But Christians have forgotten that the ministry of listening has been entrusted to them by the one who is indeed the great listener and in whose work they are to participate. We should listen with the ears of God, so that we can speak the Word of God.

The *other* service one should perform for another person in a Christian community is active helpfulness. To begin with, we have in mind simple assistance in minor, external matters. There are many such things wherever people live together. Nobody is too good for the lowest service. Those who worry about the loss of time entailed by such small, external acts of helpfulness are usually taking their own work too seriously. We must be ready to allow ourselves to be interrupted by God, who will thwart our plans and frustrate our ways time and again, even daily, by sending people across our path with their demands and requests. We can, then, pass them by, preoccupied with our more important daily tasks, just as the priest—perhaps reading the Bible—passed by the man who had fallen among robbers. When we do that, we pass by the visible sign of the cross raised in our lives to show us that God's way, and not our own, is what counts. It is a strange fact that, of all people, Christians and theologians often consider their work so important and urgent that they do not want to let anything interrupt it. They think they are doing God a favor, but actually they are despising God's "crooked yet straight path" (Gottfried Arnold). They want to know nothing about how human plans are thwarted. But it is part of the school of humility that we must not spare our hand where it can perform a service. We do not manage our time ourselves but allow it to be occupied by God. In the monastery, the monk's vow of obedience to the abbot takes away his right to do what he likes with his time. In Protestant community life, voluntary service to one another takes the place of the vow. One can joyfully and authentically proclaim the Word of God's love and mercy with one's mouth only where one's hands are not considered too good for deeds of love and mercy in everyday helpfulness.

Third, we speak of the service involved in supporting one another. "Bear one another's burdens, and in this way you will fulfill the law of Christ" (Gal. 6:2). Thus the law of Christ is a law of forbearance. Forbearance means enduring and suffering. The other person is a burden to the Christian, in fact for the Christian most of all. The other person never becomes a burden at all for the *pagans*. They simply stay clear of every burden the other person may create for them. However, Christians must bear the burden of one another. They must suffer and endure one another. Only as a burden is the other really a brother or sister and not just an object to be controlled.

The burden of human beings was even for God so heavy that God had to go to the cross suffering under it. God truly suffered and endured human beings in the body of Jesus Christ. But in so doing, God bore them as a mother carries her child, as a shepherd the lost lamb. God took on human nature. Then, human beings crushed God to the ground. But God stayed with them and they with God. In suffering and enduring human beings, God maintained community with them. It is the law of Christ that was fulfilled in the cross. Christians share in this law. They are obliged to bear with and suffer one another; but what is more important, now by virtue of the law of Christ having been fulfilled, they are also able to bear one another.

It is remarkable that the Scriptures talk so often about "forbearance." They are capable of expressing the whole work of Jesus Christ in this one word. "Surely he has borne our infirmities and carried our diseases . . . upon him was the punishment that made us whole" (Isa. 53). Therefore, the Bible can characterize the whole life of the Christian as carrying the cross. It is the community of the body of Christ that is here realized, the community of the cross in which one must experience the burden of the other. If one were not to experience this, it would not be a Christian community. One who refuses to bear that burden would deny the law of Christ.

First of all, it is the *freedom* of the other, mentioned earlier, that is a burden to Christians. The freedom of the other goes against Christians' high opinions of themselves, and yet they must recognize it. Christians could rid themselves of this burden if they didn't release the other person but did violence to him, stamping him with their own image. But when Christians allow God to create God's own image in others, they allow others their own freedom. Thereby Christians themselves bear the burden of the freedom enjoyed by these other creatures of God. All that we mean by human nature, individuality, and talent is part of the other person's freedom—as are the other's weaknesses and peculiarities that so sorely try our patience, and everything that produces the plethora of clashes, differences, and arguments between me and the other. Here, bearing the burden of the other means tolerating the reality of the other's creation by God—affirming it, and in bearing with it, breaking through to delight in it.

This will be especially difficult where both the strong and the weak in faith are bound together in one community. The weak must not judge the strong; the strong must not despise the weak. The weak must guard against pride, the strong against indifference. Neither must seek their own rights. If the strong persons fall, the weak ones must keep their hearts from gloating over the misfortune. If the weak fall, the strong must help them up again in a friendly manner. The one needs as much patience as the other. "Woe to the one who is alone and falls and does not have another to help!" (Eccles. 4:10). No doubt, when Scripture admonishes us to "bear with one another" (Col. 3:13), and to do so "with all humility and gentleness, with patience, bearing with one another in love" (Eph. 4:2), it is talking about this bearing of the other in freedom.

Then, along with the other's freedom comes the abuse of that freedom in *sin*, which becomes a burden for Christians in their relationship to one another. The sins of the other are even harder to bear than is their freedom; for in sin, community with God and with each other is broken. Here, because of the other, Christians suffer the breaking of the community with the other established in Jesus Christ. But here, too, it is only in bearing with the other that the great grace of God becomes fully apparent. Not despising sinners, but being privileged to bear with them, means not having to give them up for lost, being able to accept them and able to preserve community with them through forgiveness. "My friends, if anyone is detected in a transgression, you who have received the Spirit should restore such a one in a spirit of gentleness" (Gal. 6:1). As Christ bore with us and accepted us as sinners, so we in his community may bear with sinners and accept them into the community of Jesus Christ through the forgiveness of sins. We may suffer the sins of one another; we do not need to judge. That is grace for Christians. For what sin ever occurs in the community that does not lead Christians to examine themselves and condemn themselves for their own lack of faithfulness in prayer and in intercession, for their lack of service to one another in mutual admonition and comforting, indeed, for their own personal sin and lack of spiritual discipline by which they have harmed themselves, the community, and one another? Because each individual's sin burdens the whole community and indicts it, the community of faith rejoices amid all the pain inflicted on it by the sin of the other and, in spite of the burden placed on it, rejoices in being deemed worthy of bearing with and forgiving sin. "Behold, you bear with them all and likewise all of them bear with you, and all things are in common, both the good and the bad" (Luther).

The service of forgiveness is done by one to the other on a daily basis. It occurs *without words* in intercessory prayer for one another. And all members of the community who do not grow tired of doing this service can depend on the fact that this service is also being offered to them by other Christians. Those who bear with others know that they themselves are being borne. Only in this strength can they themselves bear with others.

Wherever the service of listening, active helpfulness, and bearing with others is being faithfully performed, the ultimate and highest ministry can also be offered, the service of the Word of God.

This service has to do with the free word from person to person, not the word bound to a particular pastoral office, time, and place. It is a matter of that unique situation in which one person bears witness in human words to another person regarding all the comfort, the admonition, the kindness, and the firmness of God. This word is threatened all about by endless dangers. If proper listening does not precede it, how can it really be the right word for the other? If it is contradicted by one's own lack of active helpfulness, how can it be a credible and truthful word? If it does not flow from the act of bearing with others, but from impatience and the spirit of violence against others, how can it be the liberating and healing word? On the contrary, the person who has really listened, served, and patiently borne with others is the very one who can easily stop talking. A deep distrust of everything that is merely words often stifles a personal word to another Christian. What can a powerless human word accomplish for others? Why add to the empty talk? Are we, like those experienced spiritual "experts," to talk past the real needs of the other person? What is more perilous than speaking God's Word superfluously? But, on the other hand, who wants to accept the responsibility for having been silent when we should have spoken? The orderly word spoken in the pulpit is so much easier than this totally free word, standing responsibly between silence and speech.

Added to the fear of one's own responsibility to speak the word, there is the fear of the other. At what a cost do we bring ourselves to say the name of Jesus Christ even in the presence of another Christian. Here, too, right and wrong approaches are mixed together. Who has permission to force oneself on one's neighbor? Who is entitled to corner and confront one's neighbor in order to talk about ultimate issues? It would not be a sign of great Christian insight if one were simply to say at this point that everybody has this right, indeed, this obligation. Again here the spirit of doing violence to others could insinuate itself in the worst way. In fact, others have their own right, responsibility, and even duty to defend themselves against unauthorized intrusions. Other persons have their own secrets that may not be violated without the infliction of great harm. Nor can they divulge them without destroying themselves. They are not secrets based on knowledge or emotion, but secrets of their freedom, their redemption, their being. And yet this good insight lies perilously close to Cain's murderous question: "Am I my brother's keeper?" Our seemingly spiritually based respect for the freedom of the other can be subject to the curse of God. "I will hold you responsible for their blood" (Ezek. 3:18).

When Christians live together, at some time and in some way it must come to the point that one Christian personally declares God's Word and will to another. It is inconceivable that the things that are most important to each individual should not be discussed with one another. It is unchristian when one person knowingly denies another this decisive service. If we cannot bring ourselves to say the necessary word, we will have to ask ourselves whether we are not still seeing other Christians clothed in a human dignity that we think we dare not touch, and thus whether we are not forgetting the most important thing—that they, too, no matter how old or high ranking or distinguished they may be, are still persons like us, sinners crying out for God's grace. They have the same great troubles that we have, and need help, comfort, and forgiveness as we do. The basis on which Christians can speak to one another is that each knows the other as a sinner who, even given all one's human renown, is forlorn and lost if not given help. This does not mean that the others are being disparaged or dishonored. Rather, we are paying them the only real honor a human being has, namely, that as sinners they share in God's grace and glory, that they are children of God. This realization gives our mutual speech the freedom and openness it needs. We talk to one another about the help we both need. We admonish one another to go the way Christ bids us to go. We warn one another against the disobedience that is our undoing. We are gentle and we are firm with one another, for we know both God's kindness and God's firmness.

Why should we be afraid of one another since both of us have only God to fear? Why should we think that another Christian would not understand us when we understood very well what was meant when somebody spoke God's comfort or God's admonition to us, even in words that were inept and awkward? Or do we really believe there is a single person in this world who does not need either comfort or admonition? If so, then why has God given us the gift of Christian community?

The more we learn to allow the other to speak the Word to us, to accept humbly and gratefully even severe reproaches and admonitions, the more free and to the point we ourselves will be in speaking. One who because of sensitivity and vanity rejects the serious words of another Christian cannot speak the truth in humility to others. Such a person is afraid of being rejected and feeling hurt by another's words. Sensitive, irritable people will always become flatterers, and very soon they will come to despise and slander other Christians in their community. But humble people will cling to both truth and love. They will stick to the Word of God and let it lead them to others in their community. They can help others through the Word because they seek nothing for themselves and have no fears for themselves.

When another Christian falls into obvious sin, an admonition is imperative, because God's Word demands it. The practice of discipline in the community of faith begins with friends who are close to one another. Words of admonition and reproach must be risked when a lapse from God's Word in doctrine or life endangers a community that lives together, and with it the whole community of faith. Nothing can be more cruel than that leniency which abandons others to their sin. Nothing can be more compassionate than that severe reprimand which calls another Christian in one's community back from the path of sin. When we allow nothing but God's Word to stand between us, judging and helping, it is a service of mercy, an ultimate offer of genuine community. Then it is not we who are judging; God alone judges, and God's judgment is helpful and healing. After all, we can only serve other Christians; we can never place ourselves above them. We serve them even when we must speak the judging and sundering Word of God to them, even when in obedience to God we must break off community with them. We know that it is not our human love that enables us to remain devoted to others, but God's love that comes to them only through judgment. God's Word serves humankind by judging it. Those who allow God's judgment to serve themselves are helped. This is the place where the limitation of all human action toward one another becomes obvious. "Truly, no ransom avails for one's life, there is no price one can give to God for it. For the ransom of life is costly, and can never suffice" (Ps. 49:8f. [7–8]). This renunciation of our own ability is precisely the prerequisite for, and the acknowledgment of, the redeeming help that only the Word of God can give to others. The ways of other Christians are not in our hands; we cannot hold together what is going to break into pieces. We cannot keep alive what is intent on dying. But God joins together in breaking, creates community in division, confers grace through judgment. However, God has put God's own Word in our mouth. God wants it to be spoken through us. If we hinder God's Word, the blood of the other who sins will be upon us. If we carry out God's Word, God wants to save the other through us. "Whoever brings back a sinner from wandering will save the sinner's soul from death and will cover a multitude of sins" (James 5:20).

"Whoever wishes to become great among you must be your servant" (Mark 10:43). Jesus tied all authority in the community to service, one to another. Genuine spiritual authority is to be found only where the service of listening, helping, forbearing, and proclaiming is carried out. Every personality cult that bears the mark of the distinguished qualities, outstanding abilities, powers, and talents of an other, even if these are of a thoroughly spiritual nature, is worldly and has no place in the Christian community of faith; indeed, it poisons that community. The longing we so often hear expressed today for "episcopal figures," "priestly people," "authoritative personalities" often enough stems from a spiritually sick need to admire human beings and to establish visible human authority because the genuine authority of service appears to be too insignificant. Nothing contradicts such a desire more sharply than the New Testament itself in its description of a bishop (1 Tim. 3:1ff.). None of the magic of human talents or the brilliant qualities of a spiritual personality is to be found there. Bishops are those unpretentious persons who are sound and loyal in faith and life and who properly carry out their ministry to the community of faith. The authority of bishops lies in accomplishing the tasks of their service. There is nothing to admire in the person himself. Ultimately, the craving for inauthentic authority reasserts its desire to re-establish some kind of immediacy, a commitment to a human figure in the church. Genuine authority knows, however, that all immediacy is disastrous, particularly in matters of authority. Genuine authority knows that it can only exist in the service of the one who alone has authority. Genuine authority knows that it is bound in the strictest sense by the words of Jesus, "you have one teacher, and you are all brothers" (Matt. 23:8). The community of faith does not need brilliant personalities but faithful servants of Jesus and of one another. It does not lack the former, but the latter. The community of faith will place its confidence only in the simple servant of the word of Jesus, because it knows that it will then be guided not by human wisdom and human conceit, but by the word of the good shepherd. The question of spiritual trust, which is so closely connected with the question of authority, is decided by the faithfulness with which people serve Jesus Christ, never by the extraordinary gifts they possess. Authority in pastoral care can be found only in the servants of Jesus who seek no authority of their own, but who are Christians one to another, obedient to the authority of the word.

Serve by listening
Actively Help
Support

Confession and the Lord's Supper

"Confess your sins to one another" (James 5:16). Those who remain alone with their evil are left utterly alone. It is possible that Christians may remain lonely in spite of daily worship together, prayer together, and all their community through service—that the final breakthrough to community does not occur precisely because they enjoy community with one another as pious believers, but not with one another as those lacking piety, as sinners. For the pious community permits no one to be a sinner. Hence all have to conceal their sins from themselves and from the community. We are not allowed to be sinners. Many Christians would be unimaginably horrified if a real sinner were suddenly to turn up among the pious. So we remain alone with our sin, trapped in lies and hypocrisy, for we are in fact sinners.

However, the grace of the gospel, which is so hard for the pious to comprehend, confronts us with the truth. It says to us, you are a sinner, a great, unholy sinner. Now come, as the sinner that you are, to your God who loves you. For God wants you as you are, not desiring anything from you—a sacrifice, a good deed—but rather desiring you alone. "My child, give me your heart" (Prov. 23:26). God has come to you to make the sinner blessed. Rejoice! This message is liberation through truth. You cannot hide from God.

The mask you wear in the presence of other people won't get you anywhere in the presence of God. God wants to see you as you are, wants to be gracious to you. You do not have to go on lying to yourself and to other Christians as if you were without sin. You are allowed to be a sinner. Thank God for that; God loves the sinner but hates the sin.

Christ became our brother in the flesh in order that we might believe in him. In Christ, the love of God came to the sinner. In the presence of Christ human beings were allowed to be sinners, and only in this way could they be helped. Every pretense came to an end in Christ's presence. This was the truth of the gospel in Jesus Christ: the misery of the sinner and the mercy of God. The community of faith in Christ was to live in this truth. That is why Jesus gave his followers the authority to hear the confession of sin and to forgive sin in Christ's name. "If you forgive the sins of any, they are forgiven them; if you retain the sins of any, they are retained" (John 20:23).

When he did that, Christ made us into the community of faith, and in that community Christ made the other Christian to be grace for us. Now each stands in Christ's place. In the presence of another Christian I no longer need to pretend. In another Christian's presence I am permitted to be the sinner that I am, for there alone in all the world the truth and mercy of Jesus Christ rule. Christ became our brother in order to help us; through Christ other Christians have become Christ for us in the power and authority of Christ's commandment. Other Christians stand before us as the sign of God's truth and grace. They have been given to us to help us. Another Christian hears our confession of sin in Christ's place, forgives our sins in Christ's name. Another Christian keeps the secret of our confession as God keeps it. When I go to another believer to confess, I am going to God.

Thus the call within the Christian community to mutual

confession and forgiveness goes out as a call to the great grace of God in the congregation.

In confession there takes place a *breakthrough to community.* Sin wants to be alone with people. It takes them away from the community. The more lonely people become, the more destructive the power of sin over them. The more deeply they become entangled in it, the more unholy is their loneliness. Sin wants to remain unknown. It shuns the light. In the darkness of what is left unsaid sin poisons the whole being of a person. This can happen in the midst of a pious community. In confession the light of the gospel breaks into the darkness and closed isolation of the heart. Sin must be brought into the light. What is unspoken is said openly and confessed. All that is secret and hidden comes to light. It is a hard struggle until the sin crosses one's lips in confession. But God breaks down gates of bronze and cuts through bars of iron (Ps. 107:16). Since the confession of sin is made in the presence of another Christian, the last stronghold of self-justification is abandoned. The sinner surrenders, giving up all evil, giving the sinner's heart to God and finding the forgiveness of all one's sin in the community of Jesus Christ and other Christians. Sin that has been spoken and confessed has lost all of its power. It has been revealed and judged as sin. It can no longer tear apart the community. Now the community bears the sin of the individual believer, who is no longer alone with this evil but has "cast off" this sin by confessing it and handing it over to God. The sinner has been relieved of sin's burden. Now the sinner stands in the community of sinners who live by the grace of God in the cross of Jesus Christ. Now one is allowed to be a sinner and still enjoy the grace of God. We can admit our sins and in this very act find community for the first time. The hidden sins separated the sinner from the community and made the sinner's apparent community all a sham. The sins that were acknowledged helped the sinner to find true community with other believers in Jesus Christ.

In this connection, we are talking exclusively about confession between two Christians. A confession of sin in the presence of all the members of the congregation is not required to restore one to community with the entire congregation. In the one other Christian to whom I confess my sins and by whom my sins are declared forgiven, I meet the whole congregation. Community with the whole congregation is given to me in the community which I experience with this one other believer. For here it is not a matter of acting according to one's own orders and authority, but according to the command of Jesus Christ, which is intended for the whole congregation, on whose behalf the individual is called merely to carry it out. So long as Christians are in such a community of confession of sins to one another, they are no longer alone anywhere.

In confession there occurs a *breakthrough to the cross*. The root of all sin is pride, *superbia*. I want to be for myself; I have a right to be myself, a right to my hatred and my desires, my life and my death. The spirit and flesh of human beings are inflamed by pride, for it is precisely in their wickedness that human beings want to be like God. Confession in the presence of another believer is the most profound kind of humiliation. It hurts, makes one feel small; it deals a terrible blow to one's pride. To stand there before another Christian as a sinner is an almost unbearable disgrace. By confessing actual sins the old self dies a painful, humiliating death before the eyes of another Christian. Because this humiliation is so difficult, we keep thinking we can avoid confessing to one another. Our eyes are so blinded that they no longer see the promise and the glory of such humiliation. It is none other than Jesus Christ who openly suffered the shameful death of a sinner in our place, who was not ashamed to be crucified for us as an evildoer. And it is nothing else but our community with Jesus

Christ that leads us to the disgraceful dying that comes in confession, so that we may truly share in this cross. The cross of Jesus Christ shatters all pride. We cannot find the cross of Jesus if we are afraid of going to the place where Jesus can be found, to the public death of the sinner. And we refuse to carry the cross when we are ashamed to take upon ourselves the shameful death of the sinner in confession. In confession we break through to the genuine community of the cross of Jesus Christ; in confession we affirm our cross. In the profound spiritual and physical pain of humiliation before another believer, which means before God, we experience the cross of Jesus as our deliverance and salvation. The old humanity [Mensch] dies, but God has triumphed over it. Now we share in the resurrection of Christ and eternal life.

In confession there occurs a *breakthrough to new life*. The break with the past is made when sin is hated, confessed, and forgiven. "Everything old has passed away." But where there is a break with sin, there is conversion. Confession is conversion. "Everything has become new" (2 Cor. 5:17). Christ has made a new beginning with us. As the first disciples [die Jünger] left everything behind and followed Jesus' call, so in confession the Christian gives up everything and follows. Confession is following after [Nachfolge]. Life with Jesus Christ and the community of faith has begun. "No one who conceals transgressions will prosper, but one who confesses and *forsakes* them will obtain mercy" (Prov. 28:13). In confession, Christians begin to renounce their sins. The power of sin is broken. From now on, the Christian gains one victory after another. What happened to us in baptism is given to us anew in confession. We are delivered from darkness into the rule of Jesus Christ. That is joyful news. Confession is the renewal of the joy of baptism. "Weeping may linger for the night, but joy comes with the morning" (Ps. 30:6 [5]).

In confession there occurs a *breakthrough to assurance*. Why is it often easier for us to acknowledge our sins before God than before another believer? God is holy and without sin, a just judge of evil, and an enemy of all disobedience. But another Christian is sinful, as are we, knowing from personal experience the night of secret sin. Should we not find it easier to go to one another than to the holy God? But if that is not the case, we must ask ourselves whether we often have not been deluding ourselves about our confession of sin to God—whether we have not instead been confessing our sins to ourselves and also forgiving ourselves. And is not the reason for our innumerable relapses and for the feebleness of our Christian obedience to be found precisely in the fact that we are living from self-forgiveness and not from the real forgiveness of our sins? Self-forgiveness can never lead to the break with sin. This can only be accomplished by God's own judging and pardoning Word. Who can give us the assurance that we are not dealing with ourselves but with the living God in the confession and the forgiveness of our sins? God gives us this assurance through one another. The other believer breaks the circle of self-deception. Those who confess their sins in the presence of another Christian know that they are no longer alone with themselves; they experience the presence of God in the reality of the other. As long as I am by myself when I confess my sins, everything remains in the dark; but when I come face to face with another Christian, the sin has to be brought to light. But because the sin must come to light some time, it is better that it happens today between me and another believer, rather than on the last day in the bright light of the final judgment. It is grace that we can confess our sins to one another. Such grace spares us the terrors of the last judgment. The other Christian has been given to me so that I may be assured even here and now of the reality of God in judgment and grace. As the acknowledgment of my sins to another believer frees me from the grip of self-deception, so, too, the promise of forgiveness becomes fully certain to me only when it is spoken by another believer as God's command and in God's name. Confession before one another is given to us by God so that we may be assured of divine forgiveness.

But it is precisely for the sake of this assurance that confession is about admitting *concrete* sins. People usually justify themselves by making a general acknowledgment of sin. But I experience the complete forlornness and corruption of human nature, insofar as I ever experience it at all, when I see my own specific sins. Examining myself on the basis of all Ten Commandments will therefore be the right preparation for confession. Otherwise, it might happen that I could still become a hypocrite even in confessing to another Christian, and then God's comfort would continue to be remote from me. Jesus dealt with people whose sins were obvious, with tax collectors and prostitutes. They knew why they needed forgiveness, and they received it as forgiveness of their specific sins. Jesus asked blind Bartimaeus, "What do you want me to do for you?" Before confession we must have a clear answer to this question. In confession we too receive the forgiveness of particular sins that come to light at that time. And it is in confessing these particular sins that we receive the forgiveness of all our sins, both known and unknown.

Does all this mean that confession to one another is a divine law? No, confession is not a law; rather, it is an offer of divine help for the sinner. It is possible that by God's grace a person may break through to assurance, new life, the cross and community without benefit of confession to another believer. It is certainly possible that a person may never come to know what it means to doubt one's own forgiveness and question one's own confession of sin, that one may be given everything in one's solitary confession in the presence of God. We have spoken here for those who cannot say that about themselves. Luther himself was one of those for whom the Christian life was unthinkable without confession to one another. In *The Large Catechism* he said, "Therefore when I urge you to go to confession, I am urging you to be a Christian." The divine offer that is made to us in the form of confession to one another should be shown to all those who, despite all their searching and struggling, cannot find the great joy of community, the cross, the new life and assurance. Confession stands in the realm of the freedom of the Christian. But who could, without suffering harm, turn down that help which God considered it necessary to offer?

To whom should we make a confession? According to Jesus' promise every Christian believer can hear the confession of another. But will the other understand us? Might not another believer be so far beyond us in the Christian life that she or he would only turn away from us without understanding our personal sins? Whoever lives beneath the cross of Jesus, and has discerned in the cross of Jesus the utter ungodliness of all people and of their own hearts, will find there is no sin that can ever be unfamiliar. Whoever has once been appalled by the horror of their own sin, which nailed Jesus to the cross, will no longer be appalled by even the most serious sin of another Christian; rather they know the human heart from the cross of Jesus. Such persons know how totally lost is the human heart in sin and weakness, how it goes astray in the ways of sin—and know too that this same heart is accepted in grace and mercy. Only another Christian who is under the cross can hear my confession. It is not experience with life but experience of the cross that makes one suited to hear confession. The most experienced judge of character knows infinitely less of the human heart than the simplest Christian who lives beneath the cross of Jesus. The greatest psychological insight, ability, and experience cannot comprehend this one thing: what sin is. Psychological wisdom knows what need and weakness and failure are, but it does not know the ungodliness of the human being. And so it also does not know that human beings are ruined only by their sin and are healed only by forgiveness. The Christian alone knows this. In the presence of a psychologist I can only be sick; in the presence of another Christian I can be a sinner. The psychologist must first search my heart, and yet can never probe its innermost recesses. Another Christian recognizes just this: here comes a sinner like myself, a godless person who wants to confess and longs for God's forgiveness. The psychologist views me as if there were no God. Another believer views me as I am before the judging and merciful God in the cross of Jesus Christ. When we are so pitiful and incapable of hearing the confession of one another, it is not due to a lack of psychological knowledge, but a lack of love for the crucified Jesus Christ. If Christians seriously deal on a daily basis with the cross of Christ, they will lose the spirit of human judgmentalism, as well as weak indulgence, receiving instead the spirit of divine firmness and divine love. The death of the sinner before God, and the life that comes out of death through grace, becomes a daily reality for them. So they love the other believers with the merciful love of God that leads through the death of the sinner to the life of the child of God. Who can hear our confession? Those who themselves live beneath the cross. Wherever the Word of the Crucified is a living reality, there will be confession to one another.

A Christian community that practices confession must guard against two dangers. The first concerns the one who hears confessions. It is not a good thing for one person to be the confessor for all the others. All too easily this individual will become overburdened, one for whom confession becomes an empty routine, giving rise to the unholy misuse of confession for the exercise of spiritual tyranny over souls. Those who do not practice confession themselves should be careful not to hear the confessions of other

Christians, lest they succumb to this most frightening danger for confession. Only those who have been humbled themselves can hear the confession of another without detriment to themselves. The second danger concerns those who confess. For the well-being of their soul they must guard against ever making their confession into a work of piety. If they do so, it will become the worst, most abominable, unholy, and unchaste betrayal of the heart. Confession then becomes sensual prattle [wollüstiges Geschwätz]. Confession understood as a pious work is the devil's idea. We can dare to enter the abyss of confession only on the basis of God's offer of grace, help, and forgiveness; only for the sake of the promise of absolution can we confess. Confession as a work is spiritual death; confession in answer to God's promise is life. The forgiveness of sins is alone the ground and goal of confession.

Although confession is an act in the name of Christ that is truly complete in itself and is practiced in the community as often as there is a desire for it, confession serves the Christian community especially as a preparation for participation together in the *Lord's Supper*. Reconciled to God and human beings, Christians desire to receive the body and blood of Jesus Christ. It is the command of Jesus that no one should come to the altar with a heart unreconciled to another Christian. If this command applies to all worship, indeed, to every prayer we offer, then it applies all the more to receiving the sacrament. The day before the Lord's Supper together will find the members of a Christian community with one another, each asking of the other forgiveness for wrongs committed. Anyone who avoids this path to another believer cannot go to the table of the Lord well prepared. All anger, strife, envy, malicious gossip, and conduct to the detriment of one another must have been done away with if all wish to receive together the grace of God in the sacrament. But apologizing to another Christian is still not confession. Only the latter stands under the express command of Jesus. But preparation for the Lord's Supper will also awaken in individuals the desire to be completely certain that the particular sins which frighten and torment them, which are known to God alone, are forgiven. The offer of confession and absolution with one another is proclaimed to fulfill this desire. Whenever anxiety and worry over one's own sins has become intense and the assurance of forgiveness is sought, the invitation to come to confession is extended in the name of Jesus. What brought the accusation of blasphemy against Jesus was that he forgave sinners; this is what now takes place in the Christian community [Bruderschaft] in the power of the present Jesus Christ. One forgives all the sins of the other in the name of Jesus and the triune God. And among the angels in heaven there is joy over the sinner who returns to God. Thus the time of preparation prior to the Lord's Supper will be filled with admonition and consolation of one another, with prayers, anxiety, and joy.

The day of the Lord's Supper is a joyous occasion for the Christian community. Reconciled in their hearts with God and one another, the community of faith receives the gift of Jesus Christ's body and blood, therein receiving forgiveness, new life, and salvation. New community with God and one another is given to it. The community of the holy Lord's Supper is above all the fulfillment of Christian community. Just as the members of the community of faith are united in body and blood at the table of the Lord, so they will be together in eternity. Here the community has reached its goal. Here joy in Christ and Christ's community is complete. The life together of Christians under the Word has reached its fulfillment in the sacrament.

No page to say...

Confess to each other

Break Thru to Life

Study Questions

1. In *Life Together*, Bonhoeffer alludes to the "Rule of Christ." This "Rule," he writes, may demand that Christians living in the Christian faith community may have to live and minister among their enemies. Following the example of Jesus, Christians often find their mission "in the midst of enemies." In Bonhoeffer's life the visible "enemies" were the agents of Nazi oppression. Are there Christian faith communities in today's world where Christians find their mission and work embedded "in the midst of enemies"?

2. Describing the essence of the Christian faith community, Bonhoeffer insists that "Christian community means community through Jesus Christ and in Jesus Christ." He adds that in a genuine Christian community Christians "belong to one another only through and in Jesus Christ." In what ways in the Christian community is Jesus Christ a source for the ways in which Christians become bonded to one another in a life of mutual love and caring?

3. How might the structures that Bonhoeffer incorporated in the community he directed and described in *Life Together*, and

stated as a goal in his "Preface," help to restructure and invigorate parish life in Christian churches today?

4. Drawing on Bonhoeffer's analysis, what are the forces that can shatter Christian community life in today's congregations? What can be done to counteract these forces?

5. How do the togetherness and the solitude that Bonhoeffer structured into his community complement each other in Christian community life today?

6. What are the advantages of private prayer, leader-led prayer, intercessory prayer, and meditation for one's personal contribution to the common life in a Christian faith community?

7. How do the three forms of service advocated by Bonhoeffer (listening to one another, active helpfulness even in little things, and forbearance/forgiveness) converge within one's life together in the Christian faith community? How important is each of these in enhancing one's togetherness in community?

8. Discuss the significance of Bonhoeffer's insistence that it is "perilous for the Christian to go to bed with an unreconciled heart." Likewise, his making it a rule to include the request for mutual forgiveness in every evening's prayers so that "reconciliation be achieved and renewal of the community established."

9. Discuss Bonhoeffer's statement that "a community either lives by the intercessory prayers of its members for one another, or the community will be destroyed." Explore further his claim that we can no longer condemn or hate those for whom we

pray no matter how much trouble they cause. "As far as we [Bonhoeffer] are concerned, there is no dislike, no personal tension, no disunity or strife, that cannot be overcome by intercessory prayer." Do you agree with this?

10. Why is Bonhoeffer insistent that the confession of sins and partaking of the "Lord's Supper" are essential in sustaining the mutual love expressed in one's communion with Jesus Christ and one another in the Christian faith community? How can renewal of these practices enhance parish life in the various forms such life takes in today's society?

The Reader's Guide to *Life Together* in the Dietrich Bonhoeffer Works: A Guide to Related Texts and Resources

Victoria J. Barnett, General Editor

The seventeen volumes of the Dietrich Bonhoeffer Works, English Edition are a translation of the German *Bonhoeffer Werke*, and fall into two groups. The first group, volumes 1–8, consist of Bonhoeffer's theological writings (*Sanctorum Communio*, *Act and Being*, *Creation and Fall*, *Discipleship*, *Life Together*, *Ethics*) and two volumes of prison writings, *Fiction from Tegel Prison* and *Letters and Papers from Prison*. The second group, volumes 9–16, are important companions to the theological works. They consist of correspondence, lectures, sermons, and other texts that give broader insight into Bonhoeffer's life and historical context during the periods in which he wrote his theological works. These are organized chronologically, beginning with Bonhoeffer's youth and education and concluding with the period of his imprisonment and death.

There are many helpful resources in the scholarly edition of the Dietrich Bonhoeffer Works, which is available in both hardcover and paperback. Each volume is extensively annotated by footnotes to the text and includes a substantial introduction written by the editor of the English volume, as well as an afterword written by the editor of the corresponding German volume. In addition, each volume provides biographical, historical, and theological information in the appendixes, along with a chronology, a bibliography, and indexes. There are also page references to the German original throughout.

Chronologically, the companion volumes for *Life Together* are volume 14, *Theological Education at Finkenwalde: 1935 to 1937*, and volume 15, *Theological Education Underground: 1937-1939* (which begins with the Gestapo's closing of Finkenwalde in September 1938 and traces the subsequent development of the underground pastorates, during which Bonhoeffer continued to mentor his seminarians illegally, up to the early months of 1940 when he was drawn into resistance circles). The historical period spanned by volumes 14 and 15 included the intensified persecution of German Jews, growing pressures on radical Confessing Church circles, Bonhoeffer's brief dramatic return to New York in the summer of 1939, the beginning of the Second World War, and the resulting dissolution of the community of seminarians whom Bonhoeffer had trained, since most of them were conscripted into the German army. These two volumes give a vivid picture of the mounting pressures on these young seminarians and on Bonhoeffer himself as he pushed his students to remain loyal to the Confessing Church and waged his own battles with the increasingly weak Confessing Church leadership.

On the surface, *Life Together* gives little evidence of these dramatic developments, yet that in itself offers some insight into the importance Bonhoeffer placed on spiritual discipline and fellowship for those entering the Christian ministry in Nazi Germany. Bonhoeffer understood that he was training his seminarians for the pastoral ministry in a totalitarian state. If they were to withstand the challenges they would face, they would need the inner strength nurtured by regular spiritual discipline as well as the external solidarity of one another.

While volumes 14 and 15 give the immediate historical context for *Life Together*, there are numerous places throughout the Bonhoeffer Works volumes where Bonhoeffer writes about Christian community and the importance of devotional and spiritual life. As editor Geffrey B. Kelly notes in his introduction to this volume, Bonhoeffer's reflections on the centrality of a spiritually grounded Christian community form a continuum that can be traced throughout his writings, beginning with his dissertation, *Sanctorum Communio* (volume 1) which describes the existence of Christ, and therefore the church of Christ, as existing in the world as the community of believers who were living for others. His exploration of the theological and philosophical consequences of this was explicated in *Act and Being* (volume 2). *Creation and Fall* (volume 3), a "theological exposition of Genesis 1–3," further developed these concepts both Christologically and in terms of what they meant for human identity.

Readers interested in exploring the evolution of Bonhoeffer's interest in creating a monastic community and his focus on spiritual discipline, daily prayer, confession, and devotional reading, will find relevant material particularly in volume 13, *London: 1933-1935*, which documents the time of his ministry in London. During this period Bonhoeffer visited different monastic communities in England, especially once he knew he would be responsible for directing the preachers' seminary in Brandenburg. Bonhoeffer Works volumes 13 and 14 (*Theological Education at Finkenwalde:*

1935-1937) document the crystallization of Bonhoeffer's personal sense of ministry as vocation. During the Finkenwalde years Bonhoeffer reflected in a 1936 letter to Elisabeth Zinn on his own turning point years earlier, the moment in which he began to take his identity as a Christian seriously: "It became clear to me that the life of a servant of Jesus Christ must belong to the church, and step-by-step it became clearer to me how far it must go. . . . My vocation now stands before me" (volume 14, 134–35).

A central aspect of that vocation was preaching. "What would I do if I knew that in four to six weeks it were all over?" Bonhoeffer wrote Eberhard Bethge in 1941. "That is running through my head. I believe that I would try to teach theology again as before and to preach often" (volume 16, *Conspiracy and Imprisonment: 1940-1945*, 161). Many of Bonhoeffer's sermons, which appear in volumes 10 through 16, translate the lessons that he taught the Finkenwalde students into messages for the entire church-community.

There is also a great deal of relevant material in the Bonhoeffer Works volumes that chronicle the period after Finkenwalde. One of the most moving documents in volume 15 (*Theological Education Underground: 1937-1939*) is his New York diary (pp. 217–45), where he made a point of remembering the Finkenwalde community whenever he knew they were in prayer back in Germany. Volume 16, *Conspiracy and Imprisonment: 1940-1945*, illustrates how in the early years of the war Bonhoeffer continued to mentor his former seminarians through circular pastoral letters and individual correspondence, and he also reached out in personal letters to the families of seminarians who had died in battle. While his active role in the Confessing Church necessarily ended in the early 1940s, his deep sense of fellowship with his students and the church-community at large remained, and that carries through into some of the prison writings in volume 8, *Letters and Papers from Prison* (also available in the Reader's Edition series). Even in prison he continued the daily discipline of prayer and reflection that he had established in Finkenwalde, and the Moravian Daily Texts (*Losungen*) remained part of his daily prayer routine. He continued the practices of prayer and devotional reading to the end of his life, not just as personal practices but as disciplines that united him in fellowship with those outside the prison walls—and within the prison itself, through his "prayers for prisoners," which he wrote while in Tegel prison in Berlin (*Letters and Papers from Prison, Reader's Edition*, 171–75).

The scope of the relevant material throughout the Bonhoeffer Works volumes shows that the practices outlined in *Life Together* were deeply personal for him, giving us not only a portrait of the development of his spiritual journey or his sense of vocation, but of Bonhoeffer himself.

Readers of this edition who want to learn more about the theological, biographical, and historical background of the writings in this edition should turn first to volume 5 of the Bonhoeffer Works from which the translation in this Reader's Edition is taken. The Bonhoeffer Works volume includes the complete annotations, chronology, scriptural indexes, and other resources.

For readers interested in more biographical information about Dietrich Bonhoeffer, Eberhard Bethge's *Dietrich Bonhoeffer: A Biography*, revised edition (Fortress Press, 2000) remains the definitive biography. A shorter reliable biography is Ferdinand Schlingensiepen's *Dietrich Bonhoeffer, 1906-1945: Martyr, Thinker, Man of Resistance* (T. & T. Clark, 2010). Christiane Tietz's *Theologian of Resistance: The Life and Thought of Dietrich Bonhoeffer* (Fortress Press, 2016) is a theological biography.

In addition, the following works may be helpful for further study of *Life Together*:

Best, Isabel, ed. *The Collected Sermons of Dietrich Bonhoeffer*. Minneapolis: Fortress Press, 2012.

Green, Clifford J. *Bonhoeffer: A Theology of Sociality*. Grand Rapids: Eerdmans, 1999. Revised edition.

House, Paul. *Bonhoeffer's Seminary Vision: A Case for Costly Discipleship and Life Together*. Wheaton, IL: Crossway, 2015.

Kelly, Geffrey B. *Reading Bonhoeffer: A Guide to His Spiritual Classics and Selected Writings on Peace*. Eugene, OR: Wipf & Stock, Cascade Books, 2008.

Kelly, Geffrey B., and F. Burton Nelson. *The Cost of Moral Leadership: The Spirituality of Dietrich Bonhoeffer*. Grand Rapids: Eerdmans, 2003.

Index of Names and Subjects

Index of Biblical References

NEW TESTAMENT